Hoarding for Law Enforcement and Other Public Officials

Maria Spetalnik, CPO®

To Devora

It was great chatting with you @ ICD 2016

Take Care,

Maria B Spetalnik

DEDICATION

This book is dedicated to the person who has supported my efforts in this, as well as every other mountain I have decided to climb, my husband Scott. Once more into the breach…

ACKNOWLEDGMENTS

I would like to thank all of the researchers, therapists and organizers who have taken a hard look at Hoarding and who have learned that there is more to it than there appears. There are thousands of hours of their work represented here and I truly appreciate their dedication and willingness to share their thoughts with me, in person, by phone, by email or in their writings.

I also can not thank enough the clients who have worked with me through the years. They have let me into their world and shared their thoughts and feelings with me. They have been open and giving. Without their assistance I would not understand how to help others nearly as well.

PHOTO CREDITS

Most photos in this book are courtesy of Conquer the Clutter, the author's Professional Organizing company, but we also incorporated some from ShutterStock. We appreciate their royalty-free licensing and access to high quality images that complement our content. The photo on page 1 is of Dr. Stephen Beatty and is used courtesy of him and David Morgan of Murdoch University.

CONTENTS

INTRODUCTION

One day I was on a ride-along with a Police Officer. (Citizens in our county can ride along for one shift once per year if they pass a background check.) We got called out for an Assault and Battery case. A woman had been assaulted in her home so we went there to take her report. When we walked in we saw an extremely cluttered apartment. I saw the officer looking around, shocked and disgusted. Then I heard him say exactly the wrong thing. He looked at her and said in an accusatory way "What the H**L is wrong with **YOU**?" The woman scrunched back in her chair as if he had thrown a punch at her. After muttering a little bit the Officer started to ask questions about the assault but she had shut down and couldn't answer.

The end result was that the report was never filed and the assailant was never even looked for. The officer was angry she had wasted his time. Worse, this citizen is not likely to ever attempt to contact the Police again, no matter the emergency.

This was when I decided to offer a class on hoarding to our local Criminal Justice Academy. I taught this over several years to many Police Officers, Code Compliance Officers/Inspectors, Fire Marshalls, EMT's, Child and Adult Protective Services, Animal Control Officers, Housing Officials and others. The feedback from the students has been good and many have told me that they are using the techniques in the class and in this book to attain better success rates with the citizens they have worked with.

I have written this book in an attempt to share this information as far and wide as possible. I am hoping this will be able to help you get a handle on this problem and work with the citizen to achieve results that are as positive as possible for everyone involved.

There is one concept which is so important I want to talk about it even before the book starts. It is vital that you understand those who hoard rather than revile them. I hope this book will help you have that understanding.

LANGUAGE USED IN THIS BOOK

In this book I will be using language that may seem a little clunky but there is a reason for it. "My Dad's a hoarder, you have to go in and fix him!" I hear this statement and many like it all the time. Calling a person a hoarder makes it seem as if hoarding is walking around in Dad's skin. This leads to dehumanizing Dad and forgetting he has skills, virtues, a history and feelings. Instead, I will be using what is called "Person Centric Language" which means I refer to Dad as "A person who hoards" and similar phrasing which implies this is a full, functioning person who has a problem called Hoarding or Hoarding Disorder. It is very important to remember that these folks need help but are, for the most part, valuable members of society with families who love them and who they love and care for.

Sometimes I will be talking as if I am the person who is hoarding so that you can see things from their perspective. Sometimes I will talk TO the person who is hoarding so you can see how I would handle it, and sometimes I'm just speaking to you. It should be clear which voice I'm using, but if I misjudged, oops, I'm sorry.

I will also be using the term "Officer" for all Government staff who interact with the citizenry. This is only being done for easier reading and is not meant as an exclusionary term for those of my readers that are not in law enforcement.

I have defined the terms and the acronyms I use for the various agencies in Appendix 2 as some names change by jurisdiction.

DISCLAIMERS

I am not a lawyer. There are International Building Codes, but every jurisdiction has and enforces different statues and rules. There is no way I could know every one or cover them all here. This book is designed for Government employees who are attached to a City, County, State or Federal Agency, I am making the assumption that you know what the procedures and policies are for your region and Agency. Please check with your local Code Compliance Office if you need information on what the specific citation and court procedures are for your area.

I am neither a doctor nor therapist of any kind. Therapy is a wonderful tool for our clients but the goals of therapy and the goals of an organizer are not the same. A therapist may be looking for what triggers this behavior in the client including their relationships, past and present, their self talk, their medications and illnesses, etc. If I were to get mired in all of this we would not accomplish what we need to for them to improve. I work *with* the therapists to try to help the client achieve the best possible outcome.

What I have is 25 years of experience working with clients and lots of other professionals who have helped me to understand things so I can better serve my clients. My job is to keep the client in the present and to help them imagine a future without all the clutter. We set goals and figure out how to attain them.

That being said, do my clients get angry? Yes. Do they cry? Yes. Are they frustrated? Yes. Do I help them move through it? Yes. Do I also tell them that these are things to explore with the therapist? **YES!!**

Everything I say in this book is for the purpose of helping you to keep your interactions productive. Nothing I say is intended as either legal or medical advice.

All client names have been changed throughout this book.

1 WHAT IS CLUTTER

Clutter is a physical thing, a continuum which we will discuss in greater detail in chapter 3. On one side of the spectrum is a messy desk. On the other end is a hoarded home, which we will cover in chapter 7. Let's start small.

So, what is clutter?

Clutter exists everywhere, and yes – it multiplies in the night while you sleep.

Clutter is like a goldfish, it will fill any space available to it. A goldfish kept in a small bowl stays small. Put that same fish in a lake or river and you get this:

There is a similar relationship between clutter and the eco-system it resides in. With Goldfish, you have the problem of them unbalancing the waterways, cutting other species out of the food chain, stirring up the water increasing sediment and making it harder on the other fish. With clutter you have relationships that can be strained, stress as people frantically look for things, and bills late or unpaid. This makes it hard on everyone in the home and the family suffers – just like the native fish.

Everyone, OK…<u>almost</u> everyone has clutter, even if it's what I call "Pockets of Neatness Resistance."

Pockets of Neatness Resistance are the small areas in the home where things are not as organized as we would like them to be. These are places like the front hall closet bulging with coats; the last 2 inches of papers you don't know where to file; and the kitchen "junk" drawer that is taking over its neighbors. Most people have at least one of these, and many people have several. Some have whole rooms.

When I was growing up our guest room was "The Junk Room" and everything got dumped in there until we knew someone was coming to visit. Then we went in and got everything put away. This is a very stressful way to manage stuff. If we knew something was in the Junk Room we would try to do without it rather than wade in to look for it.

This is a situation many people just take in stride and they are not overly fussed about it. They just accept it and move on. If this is you, that's fine. If, however, these "pockets" annoy or upset you, it's time to fix them.

The reason I hear most from our clients about why they have a clutter problem is they decide to "Put this here just 'for now.'" What happens is that the stuff never moves from this spot and stays there forever. While a temporary holding location can work, you have to have a plan to move it to where it should be. No plan means no movement.

> # FOR NOW
> # =
> # FOREVER

Many people feel as though they have failed if their home doesn't look like it belongs in *Better Homes and Gardens*. What they need to realize is that no one's does. When those magazines set up for a photo shoot they take an already uncluttered area and remove a lot of the contents to make the place look larger and airier. This is an unrealistic way for most people to live.

Clutter can be situational or chronic. When my husband fell and shattered his elbow I had to take over his household tasks, the work he does for my company, care for him and our son, and in general double my tasks in a calendar which was already overly full. While I have planned my home to be as easy to maintain as possible, even it slipped. I had to hire one of my own team to come and help me get caught up. After surgery it still took a couple of months before my husband was able to start taking back his tasks. Had there been a bigger medical issue, or one that took longer to recover from, things could have been far worse and I could have needed continuing help. That's situational clutter.

Most people don't recognize that there is an issue building up until it is completely overwhelming. This is where they can get stuck. Chronic clutter means it's been going on for a long time – usually over a year – and the person has gotten to the point where they can't find what they need so they go and get another one. This just adds to the problem, making it harder to find other things which then need to be replaced. This is one reason I often find a dozen pairs of scissors, tweezers or similar small items in a home.

People think of clutter as a very minor problem but it's really not. It can affect all aspects of your life. Your physical health can be impacted by dust, allergens, and trip and fall hazards. Your social life is also at risk. There is an implied social contract that if a friend invites you over to their home for coffee or a meal, you will reciprocate by having them over to your home. While you can take them out instead, it's not something you can do forever. If you know you won't be able to host them, you may stop accepting invitations altogether.

In their book *Life at Home in the Twenty-first Century* the authors discuss several studies that show a direct link between clutter and depression. This is particularly true for women but even for men clutter certainly makes the symptoms of depression worse. Just the fighting about the stuff can add to depression. Clutter is also a contributing factor in anxiety disorders as the overwhelming feeling of an out of control home is constantly present. Many therapists we work with have told us that when the home environment gets more organized and clean the better the clients respond to therapy as well as to their medications.

No-one likes to feel like they are out of control or to think of themselves as a "slob" a "pig", a "packrat" or whatever other name they call themselves. This negative self talk not only makes them feel bad about themselves but reduces their ability to improve their situation. The hopelessness that can set in can make it incredibly difficult to see that there is any potential for improvement, and to live the way they think they should to be like everyone else.

2 TOP TYPES OF CLUTTER

Clutter isn't just a pile of stuff, it comes in different types. Why is this important? There are certain types of hazards, like structural damage and health risks which can be associated with different types of clutter. Also, because the things you see are the things that are important to the person you're talking to, they tell you something about them as a person and how you can connect with them. We will cover this more in chapter 13. For now, let's just talk about the kinds of clutter we see most often.

Paper

In the 80's and 90's they told us that by the year 2000 the world would have gone paperless and we would never have to cut down another tree for paper. How's that working for you?

Paper is the #1 form of clutter we see in our clients' homes and businesses. I recently read a statistic which said that over 70% of the clutter in the average office is paper. I also read that every year we cut down more trees for paper than we did in the 1960's combined. This is a huge trend and it seems to us that it's only getting worse.

When you get your financial statements you have probably noticed that there are only a couple of pages which apply to your accounts. The rest is all disclaimers the companies are required to print and send you.

Where did the whole "This page intentionally left blank" thing come from? Why do they have to waste the paper and the ink to let you know they have nothing to say? It seems like its just more regulations causing us to have more clutter.

It used to be that people would read the newspaper and if there was something they particularly liked they would cut it out. They might mail an article to a friend, or post a cartoon at work. Now, due to the ubiquity of printers and copiers, we make multiple copies of things of marginal interest, including the ads and headers, and put them everywhere. If you add in the quantity of ad materials that newspapers include in their publications and companies stuff in their envelopes with their bills, the amount of paper residing in the home becomes an overwhelming problem.

Information

Wait!! Isn't this the same as paper clutter? We're talking about newspapers and magazines here, so what's the difference?

No, information clutter is different in a couple of ways. Many people keep books, magazines, trade journals, and newspapers because they may "need" the information in them some day, not just for casual entertainment.

In many ways, people think that once they purchase a book or similar item they now <u>own</u> the information in it and they now have the knowledge it contains. Never mind that they have not read the book, the info is <u>theirs</u> and they are not going to give it away because giving away the book is giving away the knowledge.

My own mother told me my whole childhood that throwing away a book was a sin. You could give it away, or better, loan it to a friend who you specifically knew would enjoy it but you couldn't just donate it to someone who might not appreciate it. It has taken several years for me to break this habit and I still have a hard time letting books go.

In this day and age there is another kind of information clutter. Electronic. Everyone knows someone with over 5000 emails in their inbox, or 500 books in their E-reader. I am often asked why this is a problem since these items "don't take up any space". While the actual data may not take up a lot of physical space, all the gadgets you need to manage it certainly does. You need the newer, bigger hard drive, a larger capacity e-reader / tablet and don't forget all those thumb drives. Then when the info is wanted, where do you look? It could be almost anywhere. Oh, and by the way, since you could lose some of that info during a power outage or an intense burst of gravity, you need to either print and file it or store it on even more devices. I had a client with 4 full Terabyte external hard drives. He was going to go out and get another one to hold more data even though he is retired, over 80 years old and could never read it all if he had an entire lifetime to try.

And don't forget that technology changes over time. We've gone from floppy discs to Zip discs to CDs to DVDs to thumb drives and SD memory cards to portable external hard drives. We've also gone from serial and parallel cables to USB cables to mini and micro USB cables. If you don't update your storage you could functionally lose it all if your computer fails. Even if the external media is okay, you can't read it anymore. Where are you going to store all of these types of media and all of these cables? How are you going to keep them all organized?

Clothes

It is interesting to me to hear the reasons people have for keeping clothes that don't fit.

"I plan to lose 10 or 15 pounds and this may fit again."

"I need to keep a "fat" wardrobe just in case."

"Bell bottoms will be back in style any day now"

"My kids will be able to wear them in a few years"

"These are such high quality they will be good forever"

"I need to have it in every color, even though I usually only wear black."

People tend to have all these items stuffed into one closet. There are things that are stained, torn, missing buttons or just plain don't fit. This can be very frustrating when you are in a rush to get ready in the morning which often leads to clothes being piled up on a chair willy-nilly just adding to the feeling of being out of control.

Crafts

"She who dies with the most fabric wins" is a sentiment I hear often. As a quilter myself I face this problem on a regular basis. Now it doesn't matter the craft, its practitioners believe that outsiders don't understand why they need all the supplies they have. Why, I'm often asked by a quilter's spouse, do they need 15 different kinds of rulers? If you ask the quilter they will tell you what each one is for, how it's used and how they couldn't manage without it. When you think that in the past all of the same crafts were pursued with only a few tools and solid knowledge it can really humble you.

People who market to crafters leave the impression that you *must* have this item in order to be successful in creating the outcome you want. There are new tools developed every day to do the same thing the old one did but in a slightly different way. Unfortunately, almost all of us are attracted to the bright, new, shiny thing which promises to make the drudgery part of the craft quicker or more fun or the fun part more efficient so you can do more of it. It can be hard to resist.

Home Improvements

Home improvers are usually heard saying "I'm gonna...." and an ambitious new project is conceived. All of the tools and supplies needed to do the project are purchased, plans drafted or bought, books on the topic acquired, and then....nothing. Some other new project has grabbed their attention.

This person's home is littered with many half-done projects, none of which are likely to ever be finished. Wherever you look you will see started jobs – the chair that has been disassembled to be reupholstered, the dresser whose hardware has been removed with one drawer of three sanded down in preparation for refinishing.

Since each job needs its own special tools, there are likely to be many duplicates. A hammer in each toolbox, one for each job, for example. Screwdrivers also seem to be needed for every task so when they are gathered together there are often 30 or 40 of them.

Unfortunately, this person lives in a future that doesn't exist. They see things how they have the potential to be, not as they are or are realistically ever likely to be. They are not really likely to be able to add on to the single wide trailer and turn it into a mansion, but in their minds, that's what going to happen.

Collections

Collections are tricky things. One problem we have as a society is that almost anything can be considered a collection. A true collector has a limited number of things they collect. They will show off the collection and know its value. Many of my clients consider themselves to be collectors but they have so many items that they can't find most of them, aren't keeping them in good condition and certainly don't have the

ability to enjoy them. We go into more detail about collections and clutter in chapter 3.

Accidental Collections

This is one of my favorite types of clutter – there is almost always an interesting back story.

Let's pretend that it is your first day at a new job. You go into your new cubicle and try to settle in. It's a little sterile but you know you'll bring in photos or something tomorrow. Your brother sends you a congratulations card with a bunny on it. You are not into bunnies particularly but he wrote something nice so you put it out on your desk. The secretary walks by and notices the
card.

"Ooooh" she says to herself "She's into bunnies!!" Now, for your entire work life in that office you are the bunny lady. Since bunnies will do what bunnies will do, by the time you pack up at retirement, you will have boxes of bunnies to take home. Stuffed bunnies, bunny balloons, bunny cards, bunny desk equipment, more bunny themed items than you knew existed! Once you get home, you unload the boxes into the house thinking "Now I can get rid of these." Then you think "You know, I really liked working with my coworkers, I think I'll just put these in the closet for now." Remember, **For Now = Forever**. When I've been going through boxes with clients I will often hear them say that they have no idea why they have this collection but they simply never seemed to get rid of it.

We've had clients who kept the plastic hangers for nametags, paperclips, and even rubber bands that don't stretch any more. It can be very liberating to move these things out of the way of the life you want to live.

Sentimental

This can be the most difficult type of clutter to let go. Jennifer held on to every piece of paper that her father had ever written on. This included grocery lists, and phone numbers without names. There were boxes and boxes of papers she couldn't deal with. This is not uncommon. I have found that the hardest sentimental attachments to break are the ones where the other person has died. People tend to revere the person who is gone and they forget the less attractive parts of their personality. Now all they remember are good things – even those they make up in their own minds.

One day I was giving a speech and a lady in the audience asked me how to store the 9 sets of china which, as the last girl, she had inherited from her mother, her grandmother and her aunts. She didn't like any of the china sets, but she was afraid to sell them or give them away because her family members would be lined up at the Pearly Gates to kick her "butt". I told her not to worry. If that is the type of people they were then they would be on the warmer side of the gate. The concept of the "family heirloom" can be a tough one. Interestingly, often family members will get angry if you get rid of one, but they are not willing to take it themselves. They think it's *your* job to hold on to it, even if you dislike it, but *they* shouldn't have to take it.

Sentimental collectors live in a past without blemish. They hold on to baby clothes from when their 40 year old child was an infant, and they remember how perfect he was. They don't remember how bad his colic was, or how loud the smoke alarm was when he set off fireworks in his bedroom. The past was perfect.

A friend of mine had a very tumultuous relationship with her mother. They wound up not speaking but once the mom had died my friend missed her and only thought about and remembered the good times, not the ones that had strained the relationship in the first place. This is the same sort of thing that battered women go through when they keep going back to the men who hurt them because the pain they were given was in the past and he's being so good now. Rose colored glasses can look into the future and the past as well as the present.

Bargains

I can't get rid of this!! I got this dress for $5 dollars!! I don't care that it doesn't fit, isn't in fashion or makes me look 10 years older, it was a STEAL!!

Or conversely…

I can't get rid of this!! I spent $300 for this dress and I'm not letting it go even if it doesn't fit, isn't in fashion or makes me look 10 years older!!

I hear these all the time. Whichever side of the Bargain coin you are on it's a trap. Keeping clothes you will probably never be thin enough to wear again can lead to bad feelings. At a minimum, they just take up space that could be much better used with clothing you look good in, that fits and you can wear.

This model fits all sorts of things, including those items that were on sale, the ones you bought because they looked "cool", even though you didn't know what they did. This seems to happen a lot around yard and "Going out of Business" sales. I have stopped people coming out of the store and asked them what they bought and why and some of the answers have been really funny but the number one reason was that it was really cheap. Even if they didn't need the thing or know if they would ever use it, they felt they got too good a deal to leave it behind.

Future Worth

Do you remember the Beanie Baby craze and how they were going to pay for your kids to go to college and for your retirement? Now you can't sell them for a quarter on Ebay. People often buy things that they think will be worth a lot of money someday. This includes things the marketers call "collectibles" or "commemorative" like plates and coins. Unfortunately, the people who buy them hang on to them – in good condition – so there is not any real appreciation in value. The rule of thumb I was given by an estate sales company is that if the ad or the box says it's a collectible, it's not.

Future worth is also subject to changing tastes. Many of us bought silver and fine china or requested it for our weddings, and now, our children are not interested in those things. I often need to console a client who is crushed that her children don't want her mother's old china hutch. They don't care that it has been in the family since forever, they don't want it and it has no value to them.

Mark had, literally, tons of metal in the back yard which he was planning on selling for scrap someday to pay for retirement. When we analyzed the approx. weight of what had not yet gone to rust, the cost of getting it shipped to the recycling center and what he would get for it, he would clear about $4000. Sadly he had spent many times that amount to acquire the metal in the first place. By keeping this collection he killed all the grass in the backyard with the rust, and put huge divots and trenches in the yard that will cost a lot to fix when he goes to sell his home. His collection turned into a net loss, not a gain toward his retirement.

Animals

Some animal collectors are true collectors – they have a special breed that they research, they are very knowledgeable about and they have only a very few specimens that they treat very well. You might consider people that own and show their animals in this light. Many people however, fall into the animal hoarding category. We will get more into this category in chapter 9.

There is an aspect of animals that is more clutter related, the animal care items. Many people have many more animal related items than their pets can possibly use. For example, 19 collars for 1 cat; 9 leashes for 1 dog; even 5 laundry baskets of toys for 1 pet. I have one client with 2 dogs and over 20 sets of food and water bowls.

Trash / Recycling

One man's trash is another man's treasure. We've all heard that before and to a limited extent that is true. This was particularly common during the Depression years and many people were either raised during that period or had parents that were who instilled the same values in them. Yes, the truly frugal can reuse and repurpose many items many times before they are completely useless. The problem comes when our beliefs about what we are going to do with the items don't match what we actually do.

We've had clients with stacks of takeout containers, piles of pizza boxes, mountains of milk jugs and gallons of Chinese takeout sauces. They are looking for the "right" way to dispose of the items (our "saving the planet" oriented clients) or to reuse them (our Crafters). It may not get to the level of hoarding but once you have more containers than you can possibly use, you are looking at clutter. Another common type of trash clutter is when you save every paper with a useable blank side as scrap paper but don't use them as fast as you collect them.

Ben was a 16 year old client who hoarded trash, including the wrappers from spinach boxes and milk jugs. He hid them under his bed, behind furniture and in heating vents to keep his parents from throwing them out. He was concerned about how they would be recycled and until the systems improved he planned on keeping them. He talked about taking them to college with him and to his next house. He was planning on ultimately having his own junkyard to keep them in. This is not a common life plan but we often do find items most people would think of as trash in our client's homes.

Boxes

If you look carefully at the clutter, this category actually covers 3 different types of clutter. Each says something different about the clutterer.

Unopened boxes, often piled near the door or under a table are most likely caused by the shop at home people discussed in chapter 7. They get so caught up in either the joy of acquisition or the need for human interaction, even if it is just a salesman, from whom they make purchases that they don't even bother to open.

Empty boxes, either intact or broken down to take up less space might fall in to the Trash/Recycling category, but might be in the Home Improvement category. After all, you never know when you're going to need a box and I have just the right size, right over here in this stack.

Full boxes, which usually can't close, tend to be full of the stuff that a hurried or frustrated person swept off a table or counter to make room for something else. The intention is to empty the box and put things away properly, but somehow that never seems to happen.

Invisible

This is my other favorite type of clutter. Some researchers and authors use the term Clutter Blindness.

Let's imagine that you have had a bad day working in the office at Megacorp. Your boss is a jerk and your clients were whining and needy and unable to be satisfied today. All in all, a stinky day. You come home, grab the mail and go inside. You plop the mail on the counter and decide to take the night off so you grab a bottle of wine or a can of beer and go watch TV all night. The next day is just as bad. Your boss was still a jerk and you have no idea why he didn't get better overnight, and you were a little hung over while dealing with the clients which just made everything worse. School open house is tonight and you have to fight your way through the crowded halls to talk to people you don't even want to meet. Today's mail just gets piled on top of yesterday's. Now you tell yourself you will tackle the mail over the weekend when you'll have time. The weekend comes and you have to shuttle the kids between sporting events and a birthday party you didn't get a gift for yet.

The interesting part is that sometime along the way the stack of mail will become invisible to you. Yes, you physically see the pile but it no longer has the impact it normally would have, your eyes just slide past. Now when something is added to the pile it's <u>instantly</u> invisible. For some people, when the pile falls over and hits the floor it grabs their attention, but for some the pile on the floor is still invisible.

When we work with clients who hoard we will often see them walk backward through this filled house without having to look. They know where the safe spots to walk are and where the stuff has been compacted. When I go through I may hit a "soft spot" and can get stuck. The clients will also tell me that everyone lives like this and they are not particularly cluttered. The strange thing is, they really believe it because they can't see it any more.

I have been asked occasionally to send photos to a client's therapist for use in their counseling session. I have been accused of photo-shopping in clutter because now, when they are not in the space and in their routine, they actually notice it. I have taken my computer to show them the photos while in their space and they have to agree that the photos are real. This can be a major turning point in the therapy process for the client.

3 IS IT A COLLECTION, CLUTTER OR HOARDING?

When you read the paper or hear a news story you will notice that there are several terms for cluttered environments which are thrown around as if they are the same thing. I'd like to define a few of these here so you can see what the real differences are.

Someone who is a Collector

- Consciously works to improve the collection
- Displays the collection properly and usually shows it off to others
- Is willing to remove inferior items
- Knows the value of the items in the collection

An example of this would be Jay Leno. He is well known for his car collection. He will acquire junk cars, but will restore them to where they are beautiful again. He has a giant airport hanger where over 130 cars and 93 motorcycles are on display and he maintains them beautifully. He will show off his collection to news agencies, will cameo them on TV shows, has used some on a TV commercial, and he enjoys telling the stories about each. Now, most people don't have the space he does but if you collect something, you can use the space you have to display it. The important thing is that a collector is selective in their acquisitions.

I collect dragons. If I took my credit card to the mall I could come home with enough dragons to fill my house and empty my wallet. I don't do that. I have rules for my collection. I follow the rules to keep the collection under control – here they are:

- All dragons in the collection must be gifts. This means that I can look all I want at the store but I can't buy.
- All clothing, like T shirts, must fit in one section of my dresser. When it's full, an old one has to go.
- All artwork is one per wall except in one designated area where a collection I stitched is displayed together.
- All statues have to reside in my curio cabinet. When the shelves get too full, the poorer quality pieces and ones that are less important to me are given away.

One of the most interesting things about these rules is that they have encouraged my family to hunt down unusual items for my collection. Dragons that are oil lamps and breathe fire, teakettles that breathe smoke, and Poker playing dragon sculptures have joined the curio cabinet family. This has really made the collection much more fun and diverse than it would have been if I had just gone and bought what I liked at the moment. These rules may not work for some, but they work for me. No matter what your rules are, setting them and adhering to them will make it a true collection rather than a burden.

Someone who is Cluttered

- The collection is running rampant.
- The collection is not properly displayed.
- The value of an individual item is not as important as the joy of getting it.
- The collection is scattered all over the house.

I have many clients who collect things but can't enjoy them. I know a train collector who has no place to put out the tracks so the trains are all in boxes in his basement. He will sometimes go look at them but he doesn't get to use them.

Julia loves to shop for beautiful china. She eats off of her old plastic plates because the china is "too good" to use. Unfortunately, the china is also not very accessible so she can't even look at it. There are boxes of china on the very top of her kitchen cabinets, under the dining room table, in the back of the guest closet, under the beds, in the attic and in the garage. She's in her 80's and fairly frail so those items might as well not exist. She gets no enjoyment from them and they are just taking up space, money and make her living space less useable. Sadly, she continues to buy more and more and so has less and less space in the home to get around in. Soon her guest room will be so full she won't be able to get in there with her wheelchair at all.

Someone who is Chronically Disorganized

- Has been disorganized for a long period of time, with a negative impact on the quality of their lives.
- Has tried numerous self-help attempts without success.
- Expects to continue being disorganized.

There is a difference between Chronic Disorganization and a short term blip where things get out of control. I mentioned my husband's broken elbow earlier and how that affected the family. This was situational disorganization and with a little time and help things were back to normal. When disorganization is the norm, that is Chronic Disorganization. This person may have been disorganized their whole life or may have just been in this state for so long they don't know how to get out of it anymore. There is such a feeling of overwhelm that they don't know where to start or what to do. They become paralyzed trying to figure out what to do and spend hours and days making no progress while expending a lot of energy attempting to make a difference.

Chronic Disorganization has a huge impact on life. In the last chapter we talked about the effect on people's lives that clutter can have. Now, imagine it has been going on for years and you don't see any improvement. Bills have gone unpaid or have been late. Job deadlines have not been met so not only didn't the promotion happen, you may be losing the job as well. Your kids don't get their permission slips signed so they can't do school events. You can't find the things you need so you have to go and buy another causing you to spend a lot of money you don't really need to. You have to spend a lot of time looking for missing things or redoing work you can't find when you need it.

I have mentioned to people in the past that I often find the most organizing equipment and books on how to get organized in the most disorganized homes. Everyone is looking for the magic bullet that will help with whatever problem they have – weight loss, financial success, or organization. Sadly, reading a book or buying a cool new tool isn't going to solve the problem. You have to find the right solution for the way your brain works and fully implement a solution, not just hope that by owning a magic widget all your problems will be over.

Sadly, most people who are Chronically Disorganized don't see a different future for themselves. "I'm a packrat, I've always been a packrat, and I will always be a packrat" is a common feeling. Often, these clients have simply never learned other ways to do things that work better with the way they think and the way their brains function.

My mother taught me that the right way to store shoes was in pairs under the hanging clothes. Over the years I have learned over 50 ways to store shoes. If one way worked for everyone the others would not have been invented. The hard part is to figure out why one way doesn't work and what might work better.

Cathy spent a lot of money on a custom dressing room. This room was about 10 ft by 12 ft. When I was there before the work was done I saw that the laundry baskets were way in the back. The closet company came in and installed a beautiful system.

A couple of months later she called me up irate. She was complaining that even though they spent all that money on the room, her husband Tom kept dropping his dirty clothes by the door. I asked her if he had dropped his clothes there before and she said he had. I asked why she didn't have the laundry drawers put by the door and she said it was because laundry *belongs* in the back. She had assumed that once the space looked better her husband would automatically change to walking his dirty clothes to the "right" place in the back.

Once we had the laundry drawers moved to the front of their closet Tom started using them and the floor stayed clear. All we needed to do was to find a solution that could work for Cathy esthetically and for Tom functionally.

The Chronically Disorganized client assumes the problem is a personal character flaw, not a problem of which solution is best for them. My Chronically Disorganized clients also often self-identify as hoarders. While the houses can look the same and there can be some of the same mental health issues happening at the same time, there is a huge difference in how their brains work in terms of their relationship with their things and how we can help them.

<u>Someone who may be Hoarding</u>

Collects items that others consider useless such as trash or broken toys.
May dumpster dive to find items to bring home to add to the collection of "stuff".
Does not understand why others can't appreciate their collection.
Collects everything – sometimes including animals.
Cannot use their rooms for the activities for which they are intended.

People hoard all kinds of things, pets, food, physical items, and more. These things are invaluable to the owner, even if not to anyone else. They honestly do not understand why there is an issue at all.

Often these clients are very creative. They see hundreds of possible uses for everything they see. While they can envision 30 things they can use that copper pot for, they usually don't put it to any use at all and instead they pile it with everything else. Unfortunately, since the pot has so much potential, they find it extremely difficult to let it go. They feel this is at the very least wasteful, and sometimes almost criminally negligent.

We talked about Ben earlier and how he hoarded trash. His belief was that the recycling program in his county, which is a very good one, wasn't doing the recycling properly so he needed to keep these items out of the landfill until the proper recycling methods could be developed or he was killing the Earth. In many ways, these thoughts were his way to justify keeping the items when others would have told him to throw them out.

Laura is an artist and she would try to show me the beauty of a rotting tomato. "Look at all the beautiful colors and textures in the mold" and similar sentiments were intended to show me that this was a beautiful thing and that beautiful things needed to be kept. She could not understand why her family and I thought she should throw out the tomato when it was so beautiful and deserving of being kept.

This mindset can also lead to collecting everything you see. You see beauty in the everyday object so you keep it. David wanted to take me to an art show of Found Art. This genre is where you use everyday items, like soda bottles, and make art displays out of them. He thought this was a way to justify keeping all the items he had in which he could see potential sculptures. Of course, he spent all his time looking for these pieces and bringing them home, but he never put them together.

Hoarding is an intensely personal, overwhelming and sometimes crippling problem. Someone who hoards usually feels that no one understands them. Often Depression, Anxiety Disorders, ADHD, OCD, BiPolar Disorder and other issues are also present. This adds entirely new layers to the problem and explains why therapy is usually required to prevent relapses, or at least to allow for recognition of a trigger so that the problem can be managed before everything spirals out of control again.

Someone in Squalor

Lives in an unsanitary condition.
Their home is a threat to the health and safety of those that live or work in it.
Conditions include urine or feces from humans or animals; rotting food; even dead animals.

This is a fairly common issue with animal hoarding but rotting food is possible, in fact likely, in any hoarded home. Though truly bad squalor conditions only exist in about 10% of hoarded homes.

Ellen had 2 large dogs and a cat. Her back fence gate was broken so she couldn't let them out back and she was not healthy enough to walk the dogs. She didn't let any of the animals out of the home for over 2 years. When we first walked in there was 2" of feces on the floor and most of the surfaces throughout the home. There was blood, urine and feces in her bed. This was an obvious case of squalor and while it needed to be cleaned up, there was no hoarding going on.

What is surprising to most people is that you can have a clean hoard. You can also have squalor without hoarding or Chronic Disorganization. The three are independent of each other though they may overlap.

Storage Areas

This isn't really a separate category since storage areas are used by everyone, and fill a great number of needs. Patrick Clark, a writer for *Bloomberg Business* quoted Ronald Havner, CEO of Public Storage saying that "demand for storage units

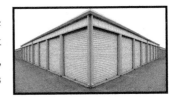

is driven by the 4 D's: death, divorce, disaster and dislocation."

Storage units, both permanent structures in storage facilities and mobile units that a facility will deliver and pick up are a growing industry. According to the Self Storage Association as of 2014 there are more than 48,500 storage facilities in the U.S., three times as many as there are McDonald's restaurants. There's enough storage space for every American to have approximately 7 square feet of storage space. The rental income is $24 Billion each year. One in ten people in the U.S. rents a storage unit somewhere and about half of us have used a storage facility at least once in their lives.

Storage areas have good uses, no dispute here. If you are staging a house for sale and there are items that will be making the move to the new home but which you don't need right now, then it's a great idea to get them out of the house so it looks more open and bright when photographed or shown to prospective buyers. If you are a business prepping for a busy time and laying in an inventory this can be an inexpensive temporary warehouse. If you are a landscaper and don't want all your equipment stored at your home but can't afford to lease commercial space, then this can be a wonderful solution to space issues. Military and business people going on a temporary assignment can rent storage cheaper than a vacant apartment.

The main concern is that, in most situations, storage areas should be a temporary solution, not a long term or permanent extension of your home. On a per square foot basis a storage unit can easily cost as much as your apartment or home. The problem is that people don't use storage with forethought. Unfortunately, this includes the Chronically Disorganized and people who hoard.

One thing I hear a lot is "I'm going to rent a storage area and we'll put the overflow in there. Then I'll go there and sort through it all when there will be time and space." What winds up happening is that once they close the storage area's door they never open the door again. Often, accumulation continues and so another unit gets purchased and another and so on.

My clients have told me that when the bill shows up they only have a few days to empty the unit before the payment is due. They say they can't go through everything in the time they have, so they will pay the bill and then they'll have a whole month to empty the unit. Unfortunately, life is busy and they forget or for some other reason they don't do it and then the next bill arrives and the same plan is made. Sooner or later they don't even bother with the rationalization; they just pay the bill and move on – often just putting the bill on automatic payment so they don't even have to see it come in.

We had a client with 5 storage units – 15' high, 15' wide and 35' deep. Once she locked the units she never went in them again. The average cost per unit was $350/month since she had rented them for so long. Now they would have been $900 each per month. She had these units for 23 years before she called us. This comes to $1,750 per month, $21,000 per year and a rough total of $483,000. Can you think of a better use of this sum of money? I certainly can. Unless you pay a premium to a specialty storage area your unit is not an enclosed and regulated environment. It is subject to heat, cold, humidity and infestation. When we finally got into this client's storage units we learned that almost everything was now trash. Ink had transferred from newspapers to the glaze on the ceramics they were "protecting". Mice and other critters had eaten their way into boxes and had nested there. Paper lice and silverfish had attacked her books. When we were done there was one pickup load of items that were worth keeping. Everything else was trash and she had to pay a junk company over $7,000 to haul it away. The grand total for this "temporary storage" came to almost half a million dollars, to store garbage. Yes, this is an extreme case but it is one that most organizers have experienced with their clients to one degree or another.

4 THE EFFECT OF TOO MUCH STUFF ON INDIVIDUALS

Excessive acquisition has a much larger effect than people give it credit for. While tiny amounts of clutter will potentially have less of an effect than a fully hoarded house, for some of these categories the difference may be negligible.

Psychological

Depression – Research by Dr. David Tolin and others has shown that clutter can actually cause depression. In working with our clients, I have seen where if depression is present, it seems to get worse the longer they spend in the cluttered environment and gets better as the space gets cleaned up. Getting organized is not a cure but it does seem to be a contributing factor for some clients.

Stress – Many people feel stress when their environments are disorganized. They can feel that things are out of control. If they already suffer from an anxiety disorder clutter can exacerbate the situation. There is an extra level of fear that other people will judge them for their home's condition.

Often people feel overwhelmed when they can't find what they are looking for. It can be frustrating and you can feel like you are slogging through Jello. Then the whole world can feel like it's falling on you since everything takes so much longer than you think it should. You may find yourself always running late to appointments so when you get there you feel unprepared and out of sorts. Stress can lead to feelings of inadequacy and lots of negative self-talk.

The Workplace

The clutter in your office can have a profound effect on your career. Sharon Mann, organizational expert and president of the I Hate Filing Club (www.IhateFiling.com), says reducing the debris-laden workplace is a way to climb the corporate ladder. She cites surveys that say half of American employers look at the organizational skills of their workers as part of the annual review process. Employers said organized workers had better chances of getting noticed, appreciated and promoted than those whose desks were cluttered.

If your boss can't see your desk he may not want to give you a choice assignment out of fear that it will become lost under the piles of paper. If you are often running late you are seen as not respecting your fellow co-workers or caring about your job in general.

Yes, some famously cluttered people, like Albert Einstein, have been successful, but there is always the question of how much further they could have gotten if they hadn't been so cluttered.

Clutter can also cost your company real money. OSHA regulations include that "All places of employment, passageways, storerooms, and service rooms shall be kept clean and orderly and in a sanitary condition." If the compliance officers determine that your clutter is a hazard, your company can receive substantial fines. Your boss isn't going to like that and you may pay the price with your job.

Social Isolation

Reciprocal invitations – Even though I mentioned this in chapter 1 I think it's worth talking about again. We human beings feel that there is a social obligation to return invitations in a similar way. If you invite me over for coffee, I'm expected to have you over to my place in the future. If my house is so cluttered that I am not comfortable having you over, I may take you out for coffee instead. This works for a while but sooner or later I will probably not accept your invitation in order to avoid the obligation and shame.

Tardiness – If you are consistently late for your social obligations people won't want to continue to invite you to events. I know people who tell their friends to arrive an hour earlier than they want to meet and are still frustrated when the person arrives late, if at all. I have noticed that while in some groups this is a running joke, this person tends not to be allowed to remain in the group as long as the others and are soon no longer invited.
Social isolation has been shown to have a huge detrimental effect on a person's health. Studies of elderly people found that people who are socially isolated are twice as likely to die early. The risk is comparable to smoking 15 cigarettes a day (Holt-Lunstad, 2010) and twice that of obesity. It also leads to an increased chance of dementia (Holwerda et al, 2012), suicide (O'Connell et al, 2004) and depression (Cacioppo et al, 2006 and Green et al, 1992). These are just some of the studies which show this is not something that should be ignored or could be caused by "simple clutter."

The Home

Water - We have had clients that have had leaks in their basements for months. They didn't realize there was a problem because there was so much stuff absorbing the water or just visually blocking the view of the water. In addition to needing to get the leak fixed, the water itself can damage your possessions and weaken the structure of your home. It also enables unwanted mold, insects and vermin to live and thrive.

<u>Dust and mold</u> – these can have devastating effects on some clients. There can be damage to the lungs that can take a long time to repair, if it ever can be.

<u>Rust</u> – Tetanus can be gotten from a cut by something rusty, but people don't seem to think that a cut by their own possession can hurt them. I've seen clients get a slice from a knife who won't do a good job cleaning it out because "It's no big deal, I know there's nothing bad on it." On one occasion I was told this in a house with mouse droppings in the same drawer the knife came from.

<u>Trip and fall</u> – especially as we age it takes much longer to recover from a fall. Many elders wind up spending the rest of their lives in a rehab or assisted living because of a simple fall.

<u>Falling items</u> – Piles of stuff can injure you badly if one falls on you. People have died trapped under their possessions. This doesn't have to be a hoarded home; it can be as simple as a bookshelf that isn't properly secured to the wall.

The Neighbors

Home Owner's Associations (HOAs) and Community Associations are very concerned about the way the neighborhood looks. This is a legitimate concern, both for friendly relations and for property values. You can find yourself being harassed or fined by your neighborhood if you don't conform to their standards of maintenance and appearance. If you start storing things in your car or outside the home you may find that you are now "in their sights" and it can have a detrimental effect on your relations with your friends and neighborhood.

In a hoarding situation, living in a multi-unit building can be of more immediate danger. The weight of the items in your apartment can break through the floor into the downstairs apartment, possibly injuring or even killing someone down there. And, any rodents or bugs will also migrate to the adjoining apartments. This can lead to huge fights involving many people. Even with detached homes unwanted guests from one house will often "go visiting" to neighboring ones. One common situation is when one home treats for mice or termites the houses around them start to find more of the pests coming into their yards and homes.

How Bad does it Get?

There are several shows about hoarding on TV right now. I am constantly being asked if they have to add stuff to the houses to make them look worse for filming. I can tell you from personal experience that the very worst of the houses don't make it on to television. Why? Some homes are so full they can't get the cameras in. They may also be so structurally damaged that they cannot allow people in to work due to a likelihood of collapse. There was one house we were called to look at where the first floor was completely detached from the outside walls and was just resting on the clutter in the basement. What would have been an even entry was now a 6" step down. In this case the county decided to demolish the home rather than to allow anyone in to empty its contents.

Actually, the worst part of a hoarded home isn't the stuff. For us, the worst part is the odor. When you add the ammonia from a pet's urine, especially from a cat; rotting food; decomposition of organic materials like paper; and spilled chemicals that have soaked into materials and floors; you get an odor that is almost physical and can be hard to handle. Not reacting to these smells is one of the hardest things my new team members have to learn. The resident doesn't even smell anything off so we cannot react or we will either embarrass or anger them. Either way the client will become less likely to accept help.

The Institute for Challenging Disorganization has worked with researchers over the years and has created the Clutter hoarding Scale. This is an internationally recognized scale of 5 categories. They are Structure and Zoning, Animals and Pests, Household Functions, Health and Safety, and Personal Protective Equipment (PPE). Each of these categories receives a rating of 1 to 5 based on severity. When working with Code Compliance or Fire Marshals we talk about what level the home is, in all of these categories. This makes it so that everyone is on the same page. I have included pictures of the booklet and the trifold in Appendix 3.

Here are some examples of the different levels of clutter:

Level 1

At this level, the public areas of the home are basically clear and organized. The clutter, if any is hidden behind drawers and doors. This is considered the standard for home maintenance and clutter. While there may be some clutter, it is quickly picked up if guests are visiting and the home is kept clean and well maintained.

Level 2

My husband compares level two to a teenager or college kid's dorm room. There may be some obstruction of the rooms walking spaces and housekeeping does not appear to be a priority or regularly get done.

Level 3

This is considered the "tipping point" between clutter and hoarding.

Clutter is preventing the use of the rooms in the way they were intended

In this picture you can see that the phone is on the commode and the water is off, there are boxes and things around it and the sink is completely full of junk. Obviously, you cannot use this sink to wash your hands, brush your teeth or do any of the other things it was designed to do.

There are often obvious safety issues such as broken glass, chemical spills, etc. that have not been attended to.

Level 4

Several rooms are cluttered to where they cannot be used as intended. In this picture, you can see the ladder to a bunk bed. The upper bunk has been removed but the child still sleeps in this bed. Usually the child is not motivated to climb up the mostly blocked stairs to this room so he normally sleeps on the couch with his mother.

Clutter usually blocks at least one of the exits, all the hallways and at least a significant percentage of the space on the stairs. There are obvious leaking cans – food, chemicals, gasoline, etc. and either you can see them or more likely, smell them.

Mold is obvious and there may be standing water or visible moisture on walls and items.

Usually this is the point in time where items start to be stored outside.

Level 5

This is the worst level. Here, none of the rooms can be used safely for their intended purposes. There are often pathways through the home that can be feet above the carpet. Boxes and clutter is normally stacked to the ceilings. Most of the home is not accessible and the client usually lives and does all of their activities in a nest. This nest if often located within reaching distance of the door as they cannot move further into the home.

I know the next picture doesn't look like much but the foot you see is mine. It is right near the railing in the upstairs hall of a three level townhome. Off to the right of the railing are the stairs to the main floor. Where you see my foot is the lowest point of the entire third level. There is only a gap of about 18 inches between the stuff and the ceiling of the main floor.

Usually the plumbing, electric and HVAC are not working and often have not been for a year or more. This may also true of the appliances (it's hard to know if they are broken or if not working due to lack of electricity) and it often smells of sewer backups

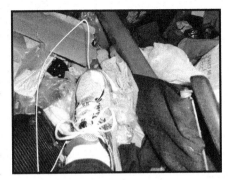

Pests are very evident and there is obvious and extensive damage to the structure of the home both inside and out.

5 THE EFFECT OF TOO MUCH STUFF ON FAMILIES

As noted at the beginning of the last chapter, small amounts of clutter can have a different level of impact than a fully hoarded home, but these issues can be present to some extent at all levels of accumulation.

One thing to keep in mind is that someone with Hoarding Disorder is not automatically a bad person, spouse, parent or child. Hoarding Disorder is only one part of a person's life. Hoarding can easily become the dominant feature, but it is not the totality of the person.

Everyone assumes that the spouse of someone who hoards also hoards. This certainly happens, but it isn't always the case. A non-hoarding spouse will sometimes add to the hoard, but they do so because they are overwhelmed and have reached a point where they see no reason to fight any more.

In some families both spouses are hoarding but don't recognize their part in it. They will tell me they have a <u>few</u> too many things but that the spouse is 95% of the mess. This can lead to fights over just who's at fault for the whole problem. Once you start assigning blame, nothing will get done to improve the situation since both people won't want it to look like the other person "won."

The hoard dominates the lives of everyone in it. The stresses it applies can tear families apart, even while they live together. This is not something that can be ignored.

<u>Time lost looking for items</u> – If you spend a lot of time looking for things, you are spending less time with your family doing fun stuff. Keeping a happy family includes spending time together where people aren't rushing around, too busy to talk, but not too busy to yell at each other.

<u>Finances</u> – Late fees, penalties and worse credit ratings can be the outcome of a cluttered environment. We have had clients that have been evicted from their homes because they didn't pay their rent or mortgage. They had the money but couldn't find the bill when they could find the checkbook. Bills can be put on a pile and immediately get lost, they can be absentmindedly tucked away, or carefully placed "so I can find it later" never to be seen again. Paying late will cause your credit rating to suffer and if collections are called in you are in real trouble. Anything you need a loan for – a car when yours breaks down, student loans for your child, even the rent on the next place will cost you significantly more, if you can get it at all.

Fear – Non-hoarding spouses usually don't know what to do and are filled with fear and guilt as they see what is happening with their children. Sometimes they simply abandon the family completely when they can't take it any more. This, of course, leaves the hoarding spouse vulnerable to even more acquisition due to the anger or grief of losing their mate. If the remaining spouse is elderly or disabled, they can be in a lot of danger. They may be removed from the home or may die early in the house.

Frustration – "He's such a slob", "She's a packrat". It's often the case that one spouse thinks the other is too sloppy and the other thinks the first is too picky. This can lead to a lot of frustration when they are trying to live together. Often this can lead to sniping at each other and can lead to breakups, even violence.

Fighting – Blaming, yelling and throwing things is not unheard of when one person is less organized than the other thinks they should be. This is particularly likely to happen if the finances are involved. We have seen a lot more fighting in homes where clutter is a factor between the family members. This is also a problem with children in the home. It is a sitcom staple that the parents are constantly yelling at the kids about their messy room. In real life though, the problem isn't resolved as quickly or as easily as on TV.

Abuse – Anxiety can run so thick in houses over the clutter, or missed bill payments that children and elders can be at risk. It does not matter whether they are at fault in any way for the actual problem; the abuser is just wound so tight they act out on anyone they can. While this does not happen in all families, it is also not uncommon.

Divorce – The end result of all that fear, frustration and fighting.

Despite all those consequences for a spouse, the largest impact of excessive acquisition is on the children. The website Adult Children of Hoarders has a lot of very good information on this. You need to be over 18 to join the blog and chat areas as the conversations can be very blunt and gritty. The sad part is that while the children truly love their parents and don't want to be separated from them, they wish people would have stepped in earlier to deal with the hoarding behavior.

Children are taught from an early age that the condition of the home is a family secret. They are warned that if they tell anyone they could be removed from the home and can lose their family forever.

There are high levels of social isolation and family conflict with rigid rules. Often, the rules protect the objects far more than the members of the family.

Their world becomes more and more limited due to the hoarding. The home becomes more and more unhealthy. Finances are used to acquire more objects, and fighting about the objects increases.

There is a decrease in the living space so privacy, intimacy and personal space become limited. It is not unheard of for the entire family to live their lives in one room. They eat, sleep, watch TV, and do homework all from the living room couch. When the living space contracts to a single point it is called a nest.

Family members find that questions of ownership count less and less. They often feel they personally have less and less value as the objects gain precedence.

Finances are so stressed that everyone is deprived of their full potential. College cannot be paid for, utilities may be turned off, social and sport activities may be denied due to inability to pay fees.

Education in how to deal with possessions is likely to be lacking. I'm talking about the skills of organizing; decluttering; discriminating an item's value vs. cost; and decision making.

All of this seriously hinders the child's ability to grow their academic and social skills. They tend to live less happy childhoods, have more difficulty making friends and fight more with their parents and siblings, if they will even talk to them at all. The more the child is isolated, the more likely they are to shut off the world and just live their lives on the couch. This is one reason why it is not uncommon to find the children living with the parents until the parents pass away. After the parents pass, this child usually is not willing to move out of the home in order for it to be sold. This adds to rifts between siblings as well.

In a hoarding situation where Child Protective Services is involved the children are usually willing to do whatever they need to do in order to stay with their parents. While not all hoarding parents fight, the fact that CPS is involved is a huge stressor. Stress alone can lead to acquiring behavior as a self-soothing activity which, of course, only makes a bad situation worse. If the parents are fighting there is usually no real progress and the children are removed. This leads to even more fights and blaming as each thinks the other is at fault for them losing the children. We have had situations where the children have been removed but the parents spend so much time fighting about fault that the children never came home.

Many people feel that hoarding alone disqualifies you as a parent. Some people have told me that the children should be immediately removed from the parents and either put in the foster care system or put up for adoption.

Some of the kindest, most supportive and most loving parents and children I know have this problem called Hoarding Disorder. The problem is treating the disorder while keeping everyone safe. When we are called into a home that is unsafe, we recommend the entire family move to an extended stay hotel. We monitor the hotel to ensure it is not being hoarded while we work on the home. Keeping the family together is better for the members of the family who can now work on strengthening their ties and supporting each other. They can attend therapy as a family and can all work to clear the home. Separating the family can add a lot of stress and anxiety which often manifests as even more acquisition and feelings of persecution and futility. If they can all work together, we have seen that the results tend to be quicker and with less damage to everyone.

6 THE HISTORY OF HOARDING AND PUBLIC PERCEPTION

Survival

Hoarding, under the strictest definition, means to gather up things as a hedge against possible future need. This can be seen in animals such as squirrels that gather up far more nuts than they can eat now to get them through the hard winter times to come.

With humans, the situation was the same. When a winter is bad or spring is late, animals are very lean and do not provide the essential fats that humans need for survival. You also need the nutrients in vegetable matter and may not be able to find them under the snow. If you do find anything it may not have enough nutrition left to do you much good.

Mankind learned to set aside food now and to preserve it so when times were hard there would be enough to eat and to keep people healthy. Today farmers set aside seed, not only enough to replant in the spring, but excess – just in case. This shows that the instinct to hoard may be very deeply rooted. When used in moderation, like for batteries, canned goods, and an extra can of oil, keeping a small excess can be a good thing.

This type of hoarding is not the same as Compulsive Hoarding but you can see why having a surplus may have been a good behavior in the past. It is only when taken to extremes that it becomes unhealthy to the person who hoards and to those around them.

Animal Hoarding

Since the dawn of civilization keeping large herds of animals has been a sign of wealth. This is somewhat less true today than it used to be, but whether you're a farmer or a cowboy, size does matter. That's the good side.

The eccentric, overdoing it part is typified by the stereotype of the crazy cat lady who lives down the street. She's rarely seen outside her home, but her dozens of cats come and go. This archetype has been found in literature for over a century.

Homer and Langley Collyer

This is a very famous case of hoarding and is here to show that this is not a new phenomenon. Many books reference the brothers and there have been many articles on them. Even today some police officers and fire departments refer to hoarded homes as Collyer Mansions. I will just give a brief synopsis about their situation here.

Homer and Langley lived on 5th Ave in New York City. They lived in a mansion their father had owned. Langley was an engineer and he took care of his brother Homer who was blind. Neighbors had been concerned on several occasions when they hadn't seen Homer for a while so they called the police. Officers went in and checked on him but there were no statutes which would have allowed them to do anything about the hoarding that was going on. Due to these strangers coming in and out of the house and the fear of thieves, Langley constructed traps in the hoard to catch these trespassers.

In early March of 1947, Langley was caught by one of his own traps, 20 feet from his brother, and died under a pile of their things. Tragically, Homer starved to death less than 2 weeks later since Langley was not there to bring in food. To clear out the house the police came in from the roof and worked their way down since they were unable to get in from any doors or windows.

There are many photographs of the cleanout available from newspapers of the time. It was a media circus with people standing out on the street all day just to see what they took out of the home. There is currently a park where the house stood and many people visit it every year.

WWII

During the war there were ad campaigns with mixed messages. You were urged to reuse and repurpose anything you could. Hold on to anything that might have another use later. At the same time, if you stocked up on things you might need later you were labeled a Hoarder and therefore you were a horrible person and very unpatriotic.

This, in my opinion, is where there was a shift from thinking that someone who hoarded was just eccentric to where it became a character deficiency. After all, the government itself was putting out ads exhorting people not to hoard and not to be like those evil, terrible folks with an extra set of tires in the garage.

Current Day

The TV shows we have on right now about hoarding are both good and bad. They are good because they are teaching people that hoarding exists but it is not a choice people are making. No one chooses to live in these conditions and to lose their families and the esteem of their friends and neighbors. In many of these TV cases there is an immediate need for a forced cleanout and the person has no choice. The show pays for all the workers, the dump fees, the therapist and gives the person money for further therapy later. Given the cost of cleaning up a situation like this, having the show come in may be the only way the person can afford the help.

The shows are also bad because drama sells. The rapidity of the cleanout does not give the person time to adjust and they are often pushed far too hard. People who undergo a forced cleanout, whether on TV or not, will often re-hoard the home within 4-6 months due to the psychological damage that's been done. While the damage would have happened anyway, the fact that there was a national audience seeing it means the embarrassment is even higher. When they do get up their nerve to ask for help again, it is much harder to get since those they turn to will see it as a useless effort – after all, the show gave you all that help and you re-junked the place. Why should I waste my time?

Every year you can find articles about someone dying in a fire in a hoarded home. This is not something that is going to go away. We need to have a better approach which causes as little damage as possible to the person who is hoarding and their families. They need to learn new coping strategies; to figure out their triggers and ways to work around them.

Genetics

There are many genetic abnormalities that can be both beneficial and harmful at the same time. There is a lot of research going on now regarding a genetic predisposition to hoarding behavior. It is believed that like addiction you could have a harder time avoiding these behaviors than the average person. This does <u>not</u> mean you will begin to hoard, but rather that you are more likely to do so than the average person.

I was recently talking with someone about this research when they told me it sounded like Sickle Cell Anemia to them. When I asked what they meant they explained that the gene for Sickle Cell is a recessive one. If you have one copy in your DNA you are more resistant to malaria. It's only when you have two that you develop the disease. A predisposition to hoard may have been good for basic survival but can also be bad if there is too much. It will be interesting to see where this research goes in the future.

7 WHO HOARDS?

I have been asked if this is an "American or First World Problem," since here in the U.S. we have a culture of acquisition. The short answer is, "no", but it is much easier to acquire things in the first world as the following shows.

The Shopaholic

This resembles a true addiction. This is the person who gets an actual rush of endorphins when they shop. For them, owning isn't as important as acquiring the item. There is often shame with the purchasing of so much "stuff." There are many tricks they will use to hide their purchases from their family but the need continues to grow and becomes harder and harder to manage.

All stores from upscale boutiques to thrift stores have their "regulars" and they buy a <u>lot</u> in these places daily or weekly and are so well known that they are greeted warmly. The shopaholic then doesn't want to return items because they don't want to be negative around their friends, the store's staff. When someone has this problem, they really need both mental and financial counseling in order to get better.

The Shop at Home Buyer

Late night TV is chock-a-block with infomercials. They promise instant weight loss, more hair, financial wealth, better health and more for a small investment in time and money. Late at night there are very few actual shows on so if you have troubles sleeping or do shift work you are likely to watch. Sadly, as we age or if we are depressed we often have our days "flip" so we are up all night and nap all day. This puts temptation front and center.

There are also the 24 hour shopping channels. Some specialize in certain items, like jewelry, and some have regular daily schedules for different types of items, like fashion accessories and household goods. You call in and talk with a representative who types up notes on your conversation. If you call back they use your phone number to try to route your call to the same person, but whoever answers the phone is looking at the notes of previous conversations. They ask you what's new with your daughter, or if you've recovered from your surgery. They take time with you. They're your friends. You want to call them back regularly, especially if your circle of friends and family is dwindling.

It is also important to remember that nothing looks bad or poorly made when it's shown on TV. Everything is bright, shiny and looks like they will solve all your troubles. Trish was a client who could barely stand up. She purchased two of the same piece of aerobic exercise equipment. She said she got the second because it would handle more weight. Trish was over 400 pounds and needed 2 canes to walk. She couldn't have even gotten <u>on</u> to the machine, much less been able to use it. The trouble was, the commercials made the products look so easy to use, of course they would work for her. After all, it only takes minutes a day to get the perfect body and anybody can get these amazing results simply and easily. At least that is the impression they are trying so very hard to give. Someone who is susceptible could be in real financial trouble very quickly.

The Rest of the Story

Okay, it's easier to acquire some things in the first world, and on average Americans have more stuff then other people, but the numbers for true Hoarding Disorder are the same everywhere.

I find it interesting that I will often be in a fully hoarded home and the homeowner will tell me that they are a little messy but I should see their sister, she's the one with the real problem. If I were to go to the sister, and I have, I get exactly the same comment pointing back to the original client. It's much easier to see someone else's problem than one's own.

Mental health professionals estimate that 2 to 5% of the population hoard (Lervolino et al., 2009, Timpano et al., 2011) with a much larger percentage of us being severely cluttered. This means that according to the 2010 US Census of 308,745,538 citizens we have between 6.2 and 15.4 million people who hoard. This is a global phenomenon and the percentages hold so that makes 138 to 345 million people worldwide, again from the 2010 estimates. This is not a small problem. It's a growing one as the global population continues to expand.

Many people think that hoarding is only done by an old, poor person who lives in a trailer in the woods with a washer and dryer on the front porch and 50 cats prowling the yard. Nothing could be farther from the truth.

There are **NO** indicators for a propensity to hoard. There is no way to predict who will be affected. It can be a huge surprise to learn that the professional person you know, who manages to look so put together, exits a home each morning that is full to the ceilings.

Hoarding has no relation to:

- Gender

- Race

- Social or economic levels – We have had clients who were on welfare and ones that pull down high 6 figure salaries

- Education level – Some clients have no High School education, some have multiple Doctoral degrees

- Intelligence – Moderate retardation to extremely well known for their high intelligence

- Age – while most people who are found out are older adults, studies show that hoarding actually starts to manifest during the teen years.

  I think the main reason that the older folks are "caught" is because they can no longer physically manage to get through their space. If they fall EMTs are often called in to get them out and then they are on the County or City's radar. Younger people have parents clearing them out or spouses who clean up after them. Once the cleaning spouse leaves or dies, the house will quickly fill. Even if they live alone, they are more physically fit and able to squeeze through and dodge past the obstructions.

- Marital Status – It is not uncommon to find that both people in the relationship hoard. They both often blame the other for making most of the mess but they will cover for them as well. In some cases, only one of the people has an issue with stuff and the other one does not. Sometimes the neater one will throw out the possessions of the hoarding spouse but in other cases they simply put up with the mess in order to be with the person.

- Children – There may be no children or many in the home. You usually can't tell that they live in these horrible conditions because they are taught at an early age to mask the problems.

The most important thing to remember about the people who hoard is that you can't make any assumptions about them. Your best option is to assume they are the smartest person in the room and they will argue circles around you if you allow it. You simply need to be clear about what you want and what your expectations are.

8 HOW DOES IT START?

When I started working as a Professional Organizer most people thought that clutter problems were created by how you were brought up. "My parents were packrats and I am too." It is the age old question of environment versus heredity. Opinions about hoarding have changed in the last decade or so. Now research has determined that true Hoarding Disorder is a brain-based problem with many potential causes.

Genetics

We mentioned that there is a genetic predisposition to hoard, just like there is for alcoholism and drug abuse. In fact, it is not uncommon to find that any given client will have more than one of these ways of self-soothing themselves.

Traumatic Brain Injury (TBI)

There was the famous case of a man named Phineas Gage. He was considered to be a hard working, responsible, shrewd businessman who was popular with the men who worked for him. After an accident sent a railroad spike through his head he was surly and profane; a drunkard who created conflicting plans that he never executed; and was obstinate while vacillating a lot. He also started to acquire vast quantities of "stuff", which he had never done before. Seven years after his death by epilepsy his body was exhumed and his skull studied. It is believed that the damage to his prefrontal cortex – on the left side at least – had been roughly the equivalent to a frontal lobotomy. This was one of the first cases leading neurologists to consider that frontal lobe damage could alter personality and affect social skills.

Recent research has shown the Prefrontal Cortex in particular is where the Executive Order Functions are accomplished and damage in that area can lead to many issues including hoarding behavior. When a person's ability to make decisions is impaired it is often the case that a fear of making the wrong decision will lead to making no decision at all.

Perfectionism

I have seen people's jaws drop when I mention that hoarding and perfectionism can be side by side. There is an assumption that if someone is a perfectionist then everything will be

<u>ultra</u> organized. This is often the opposite of reality.

Let's imagine you have a stack of papers 2 to 3 inches thick. Your plan is to file those papers so that you can retrieve them later. The average person will sort the piles into a few categories such as Insurance and then a subcategory of Life Insurance. You will then put all the papers related to life insurance into that one file folder. Someone who is a perfectionist MUST find exactly the right place to put it, often having only one page in a file so they may wind up with 50 different categories for the papers. This person may have to file the latest life insurance bill under something like: Life Insurance Bill for Mike from Travelers for Mary to use to pay off the house. The policy will have a different name and will probably be stored somewhere else. This means there can be thousands of file folders in piles because he's not sure how to file them and he can't remember the title he gave the folder if he even labeled it in the first place. People with perfectionist tendencies are very commonly going to have thousands of pieces of paper to be filed, just as soon as they figure out the exact way to do it. Everything is in the pile "just for now". Remember that For Now = Forever.

Comorbid Disorders

We will discuss these more later but if you have any of the mental illnesses that make decision-making more difficult for you, you may choose not to make any decision at all. This can easily lead to a hoarded home.

9 HOW IS THE HOARDING PERSON'S THINKING DIFFERENT FROM EVERYONE ELSE'S?

People often tell me that they don't understand how someone can live in a hoarded environment. "Don't they see that this is crazy?" In many ways, they don't. To them, this is a normal way to live and they don't understand why you have an issue with them.

The Pizza Analogy

Mmmmm, doesn't this look appetizing? Most people would say "NO!!! Throw it out!!!" but you don't think the way some of my clients do.

One client told me that if we threw out her moldy pizza she would die. To the average person this makes no sense. Let's follow the logic train she took me on:

- I'm 68 years old.
- If I lose my job I am not likely to be able to get another.
- If I don't have a job there won't be any money coming in.
- Without money I can't buy food.
- If I can't buy food, I have to eat what I have.
- Yes, there is a chance that this pizza could make me sick, but if you think about it, Penicillin is bread mold so it could actually help keep me healthier. Even if it doesn't help, it won't kill me.
- If I don't have anything to eat, I will certainly starve.
- Therefore, if I throw this away, I will die.

Unfortunately, this is a very intelligent person so her logic is solid and each step is a small one. My job was to give her an alternate but <u>equally logical</u> path that would lead to a healthier outcome.

While not all clients are this way about moldy food, the concept holds true for most of their possessions. The feeling that something bad, possibly including death, will result from getting rid of an item is very common. "If I give away my wedding dress my husband will leave me." "If I throw out this receipt I'll be audited and without it the IRS will take my house away."

Proxy by Item / Emotion Transference

The people in our lives, spouses, children and friends, have the annoying habit of not agreeing with everything we say. They are not always thrilled to see us. They have bad days they want to share with us, and are not always 100% supportive. Maybe they aren't willing to listen enthusiastically the 5th time we complain about the way the boss treated us at the office party. This is really annoying of them.

There is a possible solution for this problem. Stuff. Dolls, toys and hobby equipment may stand in for the people in the client's life who are no longer present, either by death or disenfranchisement. A doll will never argue with you, and is always happy to see you, at least in your mind. They don't have opinions that are different from yours and they always support you. They will listen to you for hours without interruption – unlike my husband.

Unfortunately, since these items are so supportive, the client can end up investing their emotions and time into these instead of in the humans in their lives. It is not unusual for the client to ignore their spouse in favor of lavishing their time on the dolls. One client had a doll hospital where she repaired them with the stated goal of donating them. She would get them up in the morning and dress them, "feed" them, and converse with them until it was time to put them in their pajamas for the night. Unfortunately, she could never let them go so, they just added to the clutter.

An advantage to collecting items instead of pets is that they will never die and never leave you.

Safety

Stuff can act as a barrier to the world. I was at a lecture by a therapist who told the story of a childhood rape victim. The girl had been taken to a specific part of the basement and repeatedly abused. She was never permitted to go to school or leave the home. When she was an adult, she inherited the home and continued to live there. She started acquiring things and created barricades between that area of the basement and the outside world. The physical barriers were for her safety. After all, if someone can't get to you, they can't hurt you.

There are also people who have suffered other kinds of loss, such as death of a loved one, divorce, and even the "betrayal" of a child growing up and moving away. These people build walls to keep people out, cocoons to keep them safe. If you don't open your doors and your heart, you can't get hurt.

There is also the fear that you will need these items someday and so having them on hand makes you feel more comfortable and safe. It is a way to make sure that as many possible future situations are covered – when something happens, you will be ready.

Persecution by Others

It is not uncommon for our clients to feel they are being singled out. They believe someone, and they often think they know who, called in Code or APS simply because they don't like the homeowner. They will tell me "My neighbor doesn't like me, that's why they turned me in." Or "My brother-in-law wants to steal my house and is working with the county to take it from me." They will assume this is because of a personal grudge and not because there is a real health and safety issue.

Right to Live as I Like

This is a refrain we hear all the time in one way or another. "I am a grown adult and a citizen of the United States and I have the right to live as I like. Nobody has the right to tell me what I can and can't do on my own property!!!" They often don't see any public safety concerns and even if there could possibly be one, they believe the Constitution prevents the government from infringing on their property rights. They are incorrect, but will often not acknowledge that possibility since it doesn't further their cause.

Everyone Lives Like This

The client really believes they are not unusual. They will tell me that if I go into any of the other houses on their street I will see that everyone lives like this. They don't know why they are being picked on.

You have to remember, they may have grown up in this environment and the rest of their family may be the same way. This validates the idea that they are the normal ones and they don't think it's fair to be singled out.

They will also often bring up family members. "If you think this is bad you should see my sister's house."

Because "Everyone lives like this" they don't feel they should have to change, the County should just leave them alone. The government certainly shouldn't be able to say they must get rid of those precious items they are storing in their back yard.

If you remember, we discussed invisible clutter in Chapter 2. This may be a situation where they honestly don't see the clutter. It could also be the case that this reasoning is used as an excuse and there is some shame deep down.

Hoarding or Chronic Disorganization?

One of the ways I try to figure out whether I am looking at Chronic Disorganization or Hoarding is to check for where the stress is. The client is always stressed, simply because I am there and am looking at all their stuff. The question becomes, what brings them more or less stress than something else. I attended a lecture where the speaker (and I'm sorry to say I can't find her name to give her proper credit for the example) explained it like this:

 If I were to tell you this pillow is covered in cat urine, dog vomit, mold and mildew you would probably not want it anywhere near you. If I told you that you must put this pillow on your couch and leave it there forever, you would be highly stressed and angry with me. This is how the hoarding client feels when I tell them that we need to <u>remove</u> this item from the home. The stress and anger levels are the same. If the client is Chronically Disorganized, they will agree to let go much more easily.

Heredity

More than 80% of children raised in hoarded homes begin to hoard themselves. There is the genetic predisposition we've discussed already, but some of it is also environmental. If you have never been taught how to live in a more "normal" home, you may not know how to. There are skills which can be taught but never were. This is one of the reasons why there is a feeling that nothing can be done. "My parents are hoarders, my sister is a hoarder, and I'm a hoarder. There is no way you can change who you are, I'm hard-wired for this. There isn't anything you can say that will change things."

This is a very difficult attitude to work around, especially since there are genetics at play.

Once they get a defeatist mindset it takes a lot to jar them into positive motion. There usually needs to be an outside force applied, such as an adult child saying the client can't see their grandkids until the home is safe. It also tends to take a lot longer as they will often backslide into a "why bother" state.

Beliefs

Gail Steketee in 2003 defined 4 main clusters of beliefs that hoarding clients have that can make getting rid of possessions much more difficult.

- Emotional attachments – This specific item means something to me.
- Responsibility for objects – This item needs me to take care of it.
- A desire to control – I have to make sure this thing does what it is supposed to do, when, where and how it is supposed to do it.
- Poor memory – I have to keep these items in order to remember something.

Beliefs make the importance of the decision much higher than just the base object would. For example, if you feel that you are responsible for properly disposing of a recyclable object and you are not sure how the county would do it, you may make the decision to hold on to the item instead of letting it go, just like Ben, the 16 year old mentioned in chapter 2.

Risk

Most people who hoard are masters of the "What if" and "Just in case" scenario building. If you suggest they get rid of something they will generate, amazingly quickly, a ton of reasons why they may need this thing in the future. Some of these are incredibly far fetched, but if they don't feel that they can respond to every scenario then they are very uncomfortable. They feel good knowing that if the zombie apocalypse comes, they have 5 chain saws to fight them off. There will, of course, need to be at least 50 gallons of gas to run the saws as well. Oh, and don't forget the sharpener for the blades and all the other necessary accessories. Once they think they have the whole thing figured out they will feel relief and pleasure. Unfortunately, they are highly creative and will come up with another "What if…" and will have to figure out even more solutions to the same problem.

Memory

People who hoard have less effective strategies for organization. This is obvious when talking about their stuff, but it applies to their memory as well. They are not confident in their memory so they like to keep things out in plain sight, because "out of sight, out of mind". Unfortunately, things get piled on top and the original item is no longer in sight. These clients are sure that forgetting things will have catastrophic consequences so they keep trying to put the most important thing on top, thereby continuously mixing the important and the unimportant. This is called Churning and is one reason the client can spend all day working on their piles but not accomplish anything.

Animal Hoarding

Animal hoarding is not the same as "stuff" hoarding. The current research does not show a correlation between the two. While many of the attitudes and issues are similar, you can have one type and not the other. The biggest difference in working with someone who hoards animals and those that hoard things is that you can't take the time in an animal hoarding situation to remediate it slowly and reduce the psychological damage to the person. The animals must be removed immediately and then the person needs to be helped.

The founder of The Hoarding of Animals Research Consortium (HARC), Dr Gary Patronek defines animal hoarding in Public Health 1999 as:

1. Having more than the typical number of companion animals
2. Failing to provide even minimal standards of nutrition, sanitation, shelter and veterinary care, with this neglect often resulting in illness and death from starvation, spread of infectious disease, and untreated injury or medical condition
3. Denial of the inability to provide this minimum care and the impact of that failure on the animals, the household, and human occupants of the dwelling
4. Persistence, despite this failure, in accumulating and controlling animals

When people hear about animal hoarding they automatically assume the owner doesn't care about the animals. When people have a lot of animals that are not well cared for, there could be animal hoarding or it could be a puppy mill. Puppy mills are run as a way to make as much money off each animal as possible without spending time or cash in maintaining it. There is no emotional attachment to the animals, they are simply a commodity. Animal hoarding is quite different since it is about caring to the point of excess for animals, which usually has a large cost with no cash inflow.

For some, the collecting of pets is a way to feel wanted and needed. In particular, by something that is always happy to see you and never argues with you or has a different opinion on how things should be done. This is very similar to Proxy By Item we discussed above.

These people will usually lavish every minute they have, all their financial resources and every bit of emotion they have on the animals, often at the expense of the humans in their lives. This ultimately means that the person who is hoarding animals tends to live alone and is very isolated from friends and family.

These folk think they can take better care of these animals than anyone else. They may call their home an Animal Rescue Center, but no one who would be interested in adopting one of the animals will ever be found to be acceptable. No one else can do as good a job taking care of the pet as the hoarding person can. A favorite way of accumulating animals is to pick up strays but some animal hoarders have even been known to enter other people's back yards and "rescue" the family pets because they think they can do a better job with it.

The biggest issue is that they often can't afford veterinary care for the animals since they are hard pressed just to feed them all. This means there is no spaying or neutering, thereby creating more mouths to feed. There isn't time to train or socialize these animals so they tend to become feral. It is not uncommon to find that some have been killed or maimed by fights within the group. Wounds are not treated so the animals are often in very poor condition when they are removed. In too many cases a large percentage of the animals need to be euthanized due to wounds or infections.

10 MENTAL HEALTH CONCERNS

When is Onset?

David Tolin and his group found in 2010 that Hoarding Disorder usually begins in the early teens, ages 11 to 15. It is mild in the mid-teens, moderate in the 20's, not usually at a severe level until the early 30's, and therapy is not usually sought until after age 40.

During early life, my clients have told me that their parents were usually instrumental in keeping the bedroom and home up to a particular standard. During their 20's and 30's a spouse may be trying to keep up but may not be able to. It is also possible that the spouse has acquisition problems since birds of a feather flock together and so they may be a full contributing member to this problem. As long as there is good enough physical and financial health, the client will continue to acquire more and more.

There was a large twin study done by Lervolino in 2009. They found that girls were more likely to have Hoarding Disorder, which is the opposite of adult studies. There was at least a moderate level of acquisition, 30 to 40%. Boys were more tied to the genetics; with girls it made only a negligible difference. There was a large percentage with comorbid disorders – OCD (2.9%) and ADHD (10%). Other disorders also played a role but these are the ones most people understand.

What does this mean? It means that the problem is usually well entrenched before anyone starts to work on it. Like any other problem in this world, the longer a problem is around the harder it is to remedy.

Executive Order Function

Impairment in Executive Function appears to be one of the major problems for people who hoard. When you think of Executive Order Function, I want you to imagine a CEO of a major corporation sitting in their chair in their office. The CEO is not the one on the manufacturing line making the widget and is not the one sweeping up afterward. The CEO guides the entire company by making decisions that will lead the company to reach its goals.

If the CEO cannot choose appropriate goals, plan how to reach them and then follow the plan, your company will be in real trouble. It won't matter how diligently the widget maker works or even the quality of the work, the company will die. It is the same in the individual's life. If you are paralyzed over whether you are making the right decision, keep changing your decision, or just simply don't make one, you will go nowhere.

People forget that not making a decision is the same as making one and so they are sometimes surprised when there are consequences to inaction. This is particularly true if the decision you were supposed to make was about when you were going to pay that electric bill.

Many of our clients have either never been taught or never were able to learn to discriminate between options to decide which is the better of two choices so they vacillate between them. This can also lead to not making a final decision. The "What if" scenarios start popping up. "What if I choose option A but B would have been a better choice? What then?" This particular circle can occupy a client for months. Now imagine that there are more than two viable solutions. The agonizing over the final choice can be excruciating.

Sometimes we are able to convey the idea that having a solution that is good enough, even if not perfect, is better than no solution at all. To a client with perfectionist tendencies, this is a painful concept.

Often a client will try to implement all of the options that they can imagine. This just leads to an even more jumbled problem as they try to pick which system for which item rather than picking an over-arching system and fitting the pieces in. It's like sorting a jar of buttons. Instead of deciding to just sort by color, the client will try to sort by material the button is made of <u>and</u> the number of holes it has, <u>and</u> by what type of garment it would be best for, <u>and</u> … all at the same time. This isn't possible which means the buttons stay in piles all over the place. Half sorted, scrambled and now they aren't even in the jar any more.

Comorbid Disorders

It is very common to find other problems along with Hoarding Disorder. Having multiple mental issues at the same time is called having comorbid disorders.

Other added disorders can make it very difficult to know which problem is causing what action. For a long time Hoarding Disorder was considered a sub-category of OCD. The problem with having it under that heading is that you can have OCD and not hoard or hoard and not have OCD. It simply doesn't fit cleanly under another heading, which is why it was broken out separately.

The most common comorbid disorders we face are:

- **ADD/ADHD** – Attention Deficit (Hyperactivity) Disorder. This makes it very difficult for the client to focus on the task at hand. Without focus they flit from one thing to another and don't complete any task. Partially done jobs sit on top of others, pieces get lost and nothing gets finished. They feel that they worked all day and didn't accomplish anything. In some ways they are right, the only accomplishment was churning the pile, not a good outcome.

- **Anxiety** – One of the reasons the hoard may have been built in the first place is because of anxiety. When anxious, some people self-soothe by buying things. They may also rearrange what they have so things are in a constant state of flux. Where did they put that thing? It depends on what they were thinking at the moment they last touched it. Anxiety also makes it very difficult to discard items because this person will often have an exaggerated fear of the possible consequences of not having it. An example of this is the pizza analogy we talked about earlier. The average person will not think that throwing out the moldy pizza will kill them, the anxious one will. Even contemplating tackling their piles is often enough to send the anxious person into a state of paralysis. They will shut down and no progress will be made.

- **Depression** – No energy = no movement. The depressed individual will not only not clean up, they will often not even have the strength to care about the condition of the home. They can be fatalistic and defeatist – "I'll never be able to get all this cleaned up, so why bother trying? It's a waste of time". The downward cycle of feelings the clutter can create will lead to a lack of discarding and may even lead to more purchasing, usually from TV. Either way, it often creates more bad feelings and self loathing. This spiral just keeps going down and down. Fortunately, if you can start the spiral going the other way, success can help alleviate the depression.

- **OCD** – This is where the perfectionism piece fits in that we discussed earlier. If you have to put everything away perfectly or be a failure, it can freeze you in your tracks. It's better to do nothing than to make the wrong decision.

- **Procrastination** – I don't mean your every day, garden variety of putting off until tomorrow something you don't feel like doing right now. I'm talking about a serious problem in this case. This level of procrastination includes putting off things you want to do, things you know you need to do. This level of procrastination leads to not paying bills, not picking up the kids at school, and not planning that vacation. It can be debilitating. There is a whole realm of study going on now about the effects of procrastination and what may be causing it.

What Triggers Hoarding Behavior?

Can you have a predisposition to hoard but never do it? Yes. Can you clean up and stay clean for years without re-hoarding? Yes. Can you turn around one day and notice that your house it totally full? Yes.

Hoarding behavior can lie dormant for a long time and then suddenly switch on. Some clients will have others keep an eye on them to warn them if they seem to be "falling off the wagon" of organization.

One of the major triggers for hoarding is loss and grief. It can be the loss of a person, a pet, a job, even of an opportunity. Mathew started hoarding again after a job he had been trying to get in another part of the country fell through . His hopes had been so focused on moving to the area and doing this very creative job that when it didn't happen he was devastated. He dealt with these feelings by ordering things from the TV and not leaving his home. He had food and groceries delivered to his home, but he never bothered taking out the trash. He didn't even open all the boxes of stuff he ordered. A regular check in by a friend got him back into his therapy group and he started cleaning up again. Without this friend, he would have quickly re-hoarded his apartment.

Anxiety is another trigger. If you anticipate an upcoming event with fear, you will self-soothe however you can. Acquiring items and rearranging them fits into this niche. Fear of throwing out something you may need in the future will keep the items in the home, leading to piles and the churning of those piles.

Medications

There are currently medications being tested to help with hoarding but as I write this there are none that make a difference.

Therapy

So far, Collaborative Therapy has been found to be the most successful in helping the hoarding patient gain control and to improve their hoarding behavior. We have found that a team approach including the Client, their family, a therapist, an organizer, and possibly clergy and friends can offer a lot of support and guidance. It is extremely important for the members of the team to receive instruction on what to do and say so that they do not hinder the recovery process. If, however, everyone participates, the client will have much better odds of success.

Harm Reduction Model

Using a Harm Reduction Model has also been found to be effective in working with people who hoard. This model was originally designed to work with drug abusers but has been modified for hoarding behavior as well.

The idea is to acknowledge that some people are unable or unwilling to stop this behavior, even though it's harmful, and instead of focusing on abstinence you focus on reducing the harm the behavior causes. In this case, you would focus on reducing the amount of acquisition rather than telling the person they can never buy anything again. Given that you can stop taking drugs but can't stop buying food, this type of approach makes sense to most people.

Food isn't the only good example of necessities that can be over acquired, but not everything in a hoard is a necessity. We also strive to reduce the harm to the individual that an abrupt and total clean out would cause. The hoard wasn't built in a day, but if it gets cleaned out faster than the person can psychologically accept, then it can be rebuilt in a very short time. Our initial goal is to reduce the hoard as quickly as possible to be in code compliance. The next step is to work with the client on a change of lifestyle.

Hoarding Disorder as an Excuse

Now that Hoarding Disorder is a separate and distinct diagnosis in the DSM V (Diagnostic and Statistical Manual of Mental Disorders version 5) there are some interesting new questions.

In March, 2013 a U.S. intelligence analyst named Harwin pled guilty to removing confidential documents from his office and storing them in his home and car. He described himself as a hoarder. If he had this diagnosis now, could he claim that his mental disorder should help him to avoid jail time and fines?

What effect will a diagnosis have regarding the Fair Housing Act and the Americans with Disabilities Act? What effect will it have in the ability to evict a tenant? Or firing an employee?

Harm to Self or Others

There is a debate in some states and counties as to whether hoarding itself constitutes harm to self or others. This is the standard that the CMT (Crisis Management Team) looks at to determine if a person can be removed from the home and put under Psychiatric observation. In the areas where this is the presumption, this means that children can be removed from a home and a person could be put into a mental institution simply because the house is cluttered. Most municipalities don't use a standardized scale, so what is "too cluttered" comes down to the social worker's opinion. This can lead to uneven enforcement simply because someone is less pleasant to work with than another. By the time the case works its way through the court system it may be too late to correct any problems that may have been caused. This will be an interesting development to watch moving forward.

11 WHY DO GOVERNMENTS GET INVOLVED IN HOARDING SITUATIONS?

The Government gets involved because the citizens need to be sure they will be safe in the buildings they enter. If you knew there was no one checking to be sure that a building was built properly and there was a decent chance the roof could fall in on you, would you be comfortable going in there to shop? Some parts of the world have this problem but here in the U.S. we require a certain amount of oversight by our government so that we can feel reasonably comfortable and be safe as we transact the business of our lives.

It is the job of the Code Compliance Department to make sure that the places we go are safe structurally. This includes inspections during construction and, for our discussion, how the building is maintained. All the rules and regulations are laid out by the International Code Council (ICC).

The ICC rules are broken into many sections such as Means of Egress, Exterior Walls, and Plumbing Systems. Every few years the ICC publishes an updated set of rules. These rules are put together by engineers working independently of any government, so they do not have the force of law until they are adopted by some jurisdiction. Many countries have adopted some or all of these rules, from one year's publication or another, with or without amendments.

The United States has not adopted these rules, but many states have. The Commonwealth of Virginia, for example, adopted the rules with some amendments, but left enforcement and funding up to the local jurisdictions. There can be a large variation in population density that may figure into what codes the county chooses to enforce. In Virginia we have the DC Metro area, the Blue Ridge Mountains, long stretches of beachfront property and lots of rural forests and farmland. This means that some areas have a person or two per acre and others have thousands. Since there is a smaller tax base due to the lower number of residents, some jurisdictions just don't have the budgets and manpower to work with the homeowner to enforce all the codes. This is also a situation where the travel time and gas usage to visit one home becomes far less cost effective.

When homes are far apart there is much less of a reason for the government to poke its nose into what a person does with their property. It will impact fewer people if there are pests or if the home catches fire, so the argument of public safety has less weight. There is more sympathy for the argument that "I can do whatever I want in my own home."

In more densely populated areas and tourist destinations, you are likely to see more multi-family units and the single family houses are relatively close to each other. Here the exterior and most of the interior codes will be enforced. After all, what happens to you will now happen to all those around you. This is where the argument to enforce for Public Safety has the most sway.

Here in Virginia each county and city can amend the building code and choose to enforce the sections they want. This means that enforcement can be different 10 minutes down the road. This leads to a real mishmash of different rules with different enforcement in different places. No wonder people get confused.

Even in the counties that choose to enforce the Interior Property Maintenance Code sections, they may not strictly enforce them if you are on private property 300 feet from any other structure. In this case, they might simply note where there are hoarded homes in the police and fire systems so personnel can be warned.

If you don't already know what your jurisdiction has enacted and chooses to enforce, then you might need to ask.

Hoarding is not always obvious. While the home may look like all the others on the street, it may pose a serious threat to the occupants and the neighborhood.

<u>Fire</u>

The number one hazard of hoarding is fire. Fire is like water, it will find the easiest path. Fire can travel invisibly, following paths that lack sufficient oxygen to be visible flames. This path can be petroleum products, like plastic melted in the middle of a hoard, or even the adhesive keeping linoleum tiles attached to the floor. If you are looking at a blaze in front of you, it can go under and around furniture and pop up behind you. There are <u>literally</u> tons of combustible materials in a hoard and it's everywhere.

Due to the quantity and the composition of the clutter in a hoarded home, these fires burn hotter than a standard house fire. This is a huge safety issue for firefighters. The chemicals and wastes make for a more toxic environment as well. Fire Departments have found that if a home is hoarded they have to roll extra trucks to have a chance of getting the blaze under control. If it is a single family home the best decision may be to let it burn while concentrating on protecting the neighboring homes.

Blocked egresses will mean that anyone in the house is at a much higher risk of dying due to an inability to escape the home. The door in this picture was the only exit from the home

and it only opened 10 inches.

Often in a hoarded home there are lots of extension cords running over and under things. Not only does this potentially cause a problem of over drawing on the electrical system but walking on the wires can create a short, a spark and then a fire. This power strip is located on a pile of clothing and is 18" above the carpet. The

orange cord is connected to other power strips throughout the home in a daisy chain.

It is also very common for hoarded homes not to have working HVAC systems so there are portable electric heaters all over the home, often on and under piles of paper. In this picture you can see that the heater is surrounded by plastic bags and papers. It's powered by the red electrical cord which runs all the way down to the lower level where there is an outlet with power. The purple sleeping bag is the only bed for this 76 year old

woman.

Combustibles pile up and once a fire starts it is extremely difficult to put out. When people think of combustibles they think of newspapers, magazines and junk mail but they forget that many cleaning products are flammable and VHS tapes – yes, people still own these – and some other plastics are made of fossil fuels and burn quite happily.

If you have ever had a compost pile, you will remember how in the winter you can see steam rising from it. This is because decomposition creates heat. The paper and other materials at the bottom of a hoard will decompose and can create enough BTUs to spontaneously combust and start a fire all on its own. It can also make the fire so hot that suppression systems can't handle it, if there even are any in place and the water is working. There have been several reports that these burn SO hot that a fire department's standard equipment may not be able to put it out.

If you add in broken electrical cords under the things people are walking on, grease built up on kitchen walls and surfaces Fire becomes even more likely. Some clients will move things off a burner of the stove to cook something and then may put the stuff back before the burner has enough time to cool down. There is also the chance that items stored next to that burner may fall down onto it before it cools. You will note that in these kitchens there are also combustibles right next to the oven. Both of these owners talked about how they would bake for charity events, family dinners, etc. in these ovens.

The microwave may be completely buried so the cooling vents are blocked – often by plastic or paper bags. The microwave can overheat and sparks can fly onto the bags, or even the heat it generates can start a fire. As you can see here, the microwave is right next to the stove and there is a heavy coating of grease on every surface including the plastic bags. It is obvious that she didn't remove any of these materials while cooking. This client is courting disaster any time she makes her dinner.

There is also a threat of the firemen getting trapped in the home due to its already weakened structural condition, narrow walkways, piles falling on them and things under foot shifting and trapping their feet. It is also almost impossible to find any

residents who may need their help since one mound of fabric feels just like another in the pitch black smoke of a house fire.

Unsafe stairs

4 feet deep, is anyone here?

Disease / Illness

The second biggest threat from the hoard is disease or illness either from the mold, mildew and chemical spills that get into the air, or from pests living in the hoard. This includes deadly black mold, Hantavirus from rats, poisonous snakes, Lyme disease from ticks, and rabies from whatever that thing is that's making noise in your attic.

Structural Damage

The weight of the contents in a home can exceed the structural design of the home. The Code Compliance Officers of Fairfax County, Virginia did some tests and determined that a stack of wet newspapers four feet high had enough weight per-square-inch to break a floor joist. Why did they use wet papers? Because in a lot of hoarded homes there are water leaks the homeowner might not even know about, or if they do, may not have fixed due to fear of discovery.

If you look closely at the joists at the top of this picture you will notice that the one closest to the window does not extend all the way to the wall. There is an illusion that it does because of the grout lines on the brick but the wood does not continue. In this house you can look through the third floor ceiling and the attic to the outside. I could clearly see a flock of birds pass. There are holes in this bathroom floor that go all the way down through another bathroom and into the kitchen on the first floor.

Collapse is a real possibility here, especially when you add the weight of a fire-fighter or EMT carrying all their gear, or a resident.

In chapter 4 I described a house where the first floor was only held up by the stuff filling the basement. I went to look at the house with a structural engineer from the county and he determined that none of the joists were attached any more. This home was not emptied, it was simply knocked down and bulldozers scooped up the stuff left behind and it all went to the dump.

Lack of Basic Facilities

Many of the homes we go into don't have one or more of the basics working. There is no electricity, water, sewage, heat or AC. This can lead to some strange accommodations by the homeowner. While there are people who still use an outhouse, it is not common here in the

US, even in rural settings. However, in a hoarded situation where the sewer system isn't useable it is not uncommon for there to be containers of human waste just sitting around. Once filled, they may be bagged up and thrown away but then again, they may not be. No HVAC means working in a home that's below freezing or over 100 degrees as we try to clear it out.

Why isn't everything working? The homeowner is afraid to call in someone to fix the problem because the repairman may turn them in to the county and the home will be condemned. It's one way they can protect their stuff and control their lives.

One issue in particular about not having sewer service is that the bacteria from human and animal waste can be very dangerous. Cholera, dysentery and e-coli are possibilities, especially if there is no running water for hand washing.

Improper Food Storage

Even if the electricity is working, the refrigerator may not be. Perishables are often found in the nesting area, the place where the resident(s) spend most of their lives. Food may be rotting anywhere in the home. We had one client who had been pickling food but then piled other things on top of it. Some of the food we found was decades old.

Storage of Items in the Yard and Vehicle

When you can't put anything more in the home, you need new locations. Usually the first place you go is your yard. Plastic bins start to stack up near the back door. Maybe you buy a shed ... or two ... or three. Sometimes you just keep things in the car. You may have noticed a car full of papers up to the window line except for the drivers' seat. Odds are, the car is like that because the house is filled up. The car

is particularly dangerous because it now has more weight than it was designed to carry. In a crash it imparts more energy and therefore causes more damage to the other car than normal. There is also the danger of items shifting and blocking the brake pedal or impeding the driver's ability to steer in an emergency.

Overgrown Landscaping

This creates habitats for wildlife that may be undesirable. Raccoons, possums, rats and snakes now have easier access to the home. Ivy in particular makes an easy bridge for insects such as termites and ants, but can strangle trees and pull down walls over time. When this home is near others, there is a public health concern that those critters will carry disease to other homes and people.

Neglect of Home Maintenance

Even if we are not concerned with the structural damage caused by excessive weight, a lack of maintenance can lead to rotting floors which can injure or entrap someone. This can come from a leaky roof that has now softened the supports, collapsing the attic into the main living area. Damage to the roof also encourages squirrels and bats, which are just rats with upgrades. Rotting wood is a haven for carpenter ants, bees, wasps and termites who will all do more damage. If the house hasn't been maintained and utilities are off there could also be unseen damage such as a gas leak in the stove which you will only find after turning the gas back on or a broken water heater that will start leaking again as soon as the water is turned on. There is also the problem of a neglected house encouraging neglect from the neighbors.

There is something called "The Broken Windows Theory" posited by James Q. Wilson. It talks about a building with a lot of windows. If one is broken, and left unrepaired, soon the rest of the windows will be broken. This is because breaking windows is fun and now it seems that no one cares and no one is in charge. It is now being used as a policing strategy. If you ignore the petty crimes then the criminals  will think that they are less likely to be caught in this area. The more you get away with, the more you can do. It's sort of the "Give him an inch, he'll take a mile" approach to crime as well as neighborhood condition. It is amazing how quickly a neighborhood can decline when it appears that people don't care about their homes and environment. This is one reason that HOA's exist. Gentrification is the reverse of this process and while it can work, it takes a lot more cleaning up to improve a neighborhood than the damage needed to spiral it down.

Animal Hoarding

Most places seem to enforce a limit on the number animals a person can own, with the exception of cats. There is usually a limit based on square footage per animal. There are only a couple of jurisdictions I have heard of with a limit on the number of cats you may have. Aside from the cruelty imposed on the animals themselves, the government is concerned with the health risks posed to people in the area. The bacteria found in animal fecal matter can be harmful to humans, and large quantities of fecal matter can overtax a water reclamation system as well as attract insects that spread disease. Dead and dying animals lying around are a breeding ground for lots of diseases that can be transmitted to humans.

Impacts of Hoarding on the Community

Hoarding is a community health problem and has a huge expense associated with it. Many people balk at paying for a clean up but they don't understand that NOT cleaning it up is far more expensive.

- **Impacts on the residents**

  o Medical – mold and mildew caused by leaking pipes and water coming in from structural damage can harm the respiratory system
  o Medical – bites and diseases brought in by pests like mice, rats, snakes or insects
  o Medical – injuries from falls, cuts from buried items, infections from untreated cuts
  o Damage to their possessions due to fire, water damage, breakage from shifting piles and being walked on
  o Fire damage leading to loss of possessions and home
  o Repair fees – some pay for repairs the landlord would normally cover as a way to ensure that the landlord doesn't enter the home and see the clutter
  o The concern that if the clutter is seen they will be evicted.
  o Costs to fight eviction and to move
  o High cost of new location to live – if one can be found at all
  o Storage rental fees – many people rent storage even while homeless to make sure their things are protected
  o Duplicate items are purchased because the original can't be found
  o Phone, gas, electricity and/or water may be cut off because they can't find the bills. Getting them turned on again is costly, if they can do it at all.
  o Their clutter may prevent them from holding a job due to tardiness and decreased productivity

- **Impacts on landlords**

    o Fires
    o Pest infestations – treatments are more likely to be needed and will be more expensive due to the level of infestation and the number of hiding places making treatment less effective
    o Injuries
    o Other tenants impacted and angry
    o Eviction costs
    o Need heavy cleaning after eviction
    o Structural damage needing costly repairs
    o Lost rental revenue while repairs being made

- **Impacts on the neighborhood**

    o Fires
    o Pests migrate from one home to another
    o Decreased neighborhood property values
    o Looks bad, smells bad, dangerous – both home and yard, fosters hiding places for pests and insects like mosquitoes

- **Impacts on society at large**

    o Many people who hoard do not have insurance, often because they can't find the bills to pay for it. They may have also spent all their money on the stuff and so can't afford insurance. This means when they are sick they use emergency rooms, clogging the system.
    o Social Services need to house, feed and otherwise care for these individuals while they are recovering from a fire or some other disaster. And if they cannot find housing, they will be part of the homeless population and receive other services.
    o Once a person is homeless they may be prosecuted for crimes such as squatting, vagrancy and other petty crimes which often don't cure the underlying problem; they simply clog up the courts, and waste the time of attorneys and officers.

How to Describe What You See

One of my friends tells people that I won't even blink until there are "Multiple species of feces" in a home. What I consider to be a disaster of a home may be very different from someone else's definition. When I teach about hoarding I like to teach people to use the Clutter Hoarding Scale from ICD which is discussed a little more in chapter 4, The Effect of

Too Much Stuff on Individuals; and shown in Appendix 3 of this book. You can also download it free from the ICD site listed under Resources – Professional Organizations.

Using a common scale makes a lot of sense, especially when not only implemented in one department, but when done system wide. When the different agencies describe a home they can use the scale to ensure they are on the same page without having to go into great and graphic detail. The scale says that the highest score a home receives in any space is the number for the house. While this works, we tend to describe each of the 5 categories by room, i.e. the kitchen is a 3 on clutter but a 5 on pests. This creates a very clear picture to those discussing the problem.

What is This Going to Cost Us?

In many ways the cost depends on how early intervention happens and how it's handled. The Mental Health Association of San Francisco put together the following chart and supplied the cost estimates. This was published in *Beyond Overwhelmed* by the San Francisco Hoarding Task Force 2009. Given the time since publication, I think it is safe to assume that current numbers will be higher for most locations.

In San Francisco the costs came to over $1 million per year by government service providers and landlords. This **does not** include the costs to the individuals involved. The conservative estimate would come to $6.43 million per year, not including the cost of the lives of all those individuals and families who die.

- Pest infestations ($50 - $1.5K)
- Animal control costs ($200 - $1.5K)
- Foregone rent ($1K -$4K)
- Eviction related costs ($2K -$100K)
- Heavy cleaning ($75 - $4K)
- Evictions and repair costs ($50K - $75K)
- Fire related cost exceeding $500K

Involvement of Public agencies – $50K - $200K per client
- Department of Aging & Adult Services
- Department of Environmental Health
- Department of Public Health
- Housing Authority
- First Responders - Fire, Police, Emergency Medical Technicians
- Animal Control
- Legal Aid
- Health Clinics
- Senior Services

Private services are often needed and can be costly: cleaning and repairs, professional organizers, medical/behavioral health programs.

The main point is that any cost listed here will only go up as time passes. Not just because prices rise for inflation but because the level of damage and repairs needed also increases. A floor that is a little spongy now may be completely rotted through in 6 months.

The Mental Health Association of San Francisco also put together several scenarios to show the cost impacts of intervention to the community. These can be found in Appendix 5.

12 OFFICER SAFETY

Everyone who works with the public knows that the most dangerous thing you can do is to go into the person's home. You don't know where the exits are, what weapons could be there, or what domestic issues may turn violent. In a hoarded environment you have all of the same concerns and more.

People who hoard tend to make sure the outside of the house looks good for as long as possible. They don't want trouble with their neighbors or their Community Association/HOA, if there is one. Because of this, it may not be obvious from the outside when there is hoarding going on.

The neighbors didn't know this home was fully hoarded until the EMT's had to go in and rescue the homeowner from a medical emergency

We discussed neglect of home maintenance in chapter 11. If there is evidence the homeowner isn't paying attention to the outside of the home, you are likely looking at a situation where the inside hasn't been cared for either. There are some things you can look for that can warn you what you may be encountering inside.

If the house has blinds or curtains and you notice that some or all of them are crushed against the glass, this is a clue. This is often due to piles of possessions shifting so they are now leaning towards or against the window.

If you see a lot of exterior storage, like Pods that are rusty and look like they have been there for a long time; large tote bins; or old dressers, this is an indicator. This particular house has had a minimum of two storage pods in the yard for at least the last 10 years. Sometimes they change

companies but they never get rid of the pods. The presence of a lot of things sitting out around the house that aren't usually left outside is another indicator. This doesn't tend to happen until there isn't enough room inside to store these things. For example, if there is a garage but the bicycle is in the back yard and looks like it has been there for a while, this likely means there isn't room to put a bike in the garage.

If the car is filled with stuff, this is another indication the home may not have any more room. This car has only the driver's space open and I would expect the house to be the same.

If you don't live in an area where outhouses are common, and you don't see evidence of a construction crew, seeing a port-a-potty is a bad sign. It usually means there isn't running water in the home or that there's no connection to the sewer system. This can mean that when it's cold or rainy people may be using buckets or other containers for their waste and these may or may not be cleaned regularly.

Physical Safety

The hoarding citizen will not want you in their environment. You are a threat, more than for the average person because you will not only be an official but you will also be touching their stuff – if only to keep from falling. They will assume you are judging them, looking down on them, and you may do something drastic to them – such as throw them out of their own home. To be fair, these are often very realistic fears. Many people with hoarding issues have seen this play out in their own families before. Homes have been condemned and they were forced to move out, they may have been taken by CPS, a parent may have spent jail time for not cleaning up the house after the court got involved. That is one reason why, when you ring their front doorbell, they will <u>come around the house from the back</u>. This way you won't be able to physically see the problem so you won't have probable cause to act.

The fear of having people looking in, either to steal their things or to find reasons to report them, often leads to the <u>windows being fully blocked</u>. There have been many cases where the windows have been covered in brown paper or similar things to keep people from looking in. This is often done with newspapers or boxes as well. It may just be a covering or there could be full, heavy boxes in the windows. The goal of the full boxes would be to injure any thieves that are attempting to break in. Blocking these windows leads to a very dim interior so it can be difficult to see where there is safe footing. Children are often taught to not look out the windows, just in case someone else is looking in. When they look, they have to sneak to do it.

Piles of possessions are also a potential issue for you. While in most cases the piles are just intended as the way to keep the items, they can fall and entrap people. In a few instances however, people have intentionally structured their clutter to create traps. This may be because the person thinks that people have been breaking in to steal their things, or are likely to. We talked about the Collyer brothers in Chapter 6. Langley died in his own trap but it could just as easily have been an officer.

Many hoarded homes have what we call "Goat Paths" or "Goat Trails" which are pathways through the home. They are the low points of stuff in the room that you have to walk on. In this picture, the walkway on the left is three feet off the carpet. Because the homeowner walks these paths every day they know where the, possibly hidden, obstacles are. And because they walk the same paths the same way every day, where they step the stuff is compacted and stable. If you walk on this path you're likely to find spots that are hard and stable, as well as spots that are spongy and slippery. You are much more likely than the homeowner to lose your balance or get your feet stuck. Your best option is to pay close attention to where the homeowner steps and try to hit the same spots – even if it means seriously changing your stride. You do not want your foot caught, especially if you are already in a dangerous situation with this citizen.

Structural damage to the home can lead to many issues. According to nbcconnecticut.com there was a deadly event in 2014 where a woman died in her basement after her first floor collapsed on top of her.

In hoarded homes there are often unrepaired water leaks from the plumbing or from the outside that are never addressed, either because the homeowner didn't know there was a problem or because they didn't want to call in people to fix it. Unaddressed water issues can lead to soft spots in the floor which can give way beneath you. I have seen cases where the second floor has completely given way and is resting on the living room floor. The 90 pound resident in a house dress may not have fallen through yet but a 225 pound officer in all his gear just might. Crashing through the floor is not the only issue since you can land on hard or sharp items and then all the stuff near the hole will crash down on you as well.

Air quality is often poor in hoarded homes. There is a smell characteristic to most hoarded houses created by rotting food, animal waste, possibly dead animals decomposing, pet dander, insects, mold and spilled substances. The air quality and the smell get worse the longer the hoard is growing. Prolonged exposure to these can cause illness and disease, but since you're new to the environment even a short stay can lead to difficulty breathing, maybe even sneezing, coughing or nausea.

Egress is often blocked. It can force a confrontation and if you get into an altercation with someone, you may not have much room to move or any way out. They will also have no way out and aggression levels will often escalate. Windows are usually at least partially obstructed and even if there are multiple doors to the outside, there may only be one that works and it may not open far. One client had a front door that opened 10" and it was the only way in or out of the home. In this picture there is a basement door behind these bags. There is no way you could exit the basement except up the stairs into the kitchen. This lack of exit space also makes it extremely difficult to extract a suspect or a victim. You will have to fight them all the way through the house rather than just getting out the closest door.

Hiding

It is extremely difficult to find a person who doesn't want to be found in a hoarded home. They know all the safe paths; they know where they can hide and what is safe to pull over themselves for concealment, and where any traps are. They know where to hide items such as stolen merchandise and they know it's not worth your time to look for it if you are just suspicious. Doing a thorough search of the home's contents can take weeks and many jurisdictions won't think that the time needed to do this is cost effective and will instead just try to catch the suspect with it later.

Weapons

I went to an assessment on a home where the homeowner was in the hospital and his sister needed help to clear it so he could move back in. When I opened the door I saw on the threshold 5 different types of bullets, just lying there loose. We had no idea how many weapons were in the house, where they were located, or if they were loaded. We have found guns pointed toward doors, stuffed between couch cushions, in drawers in children's rooms and buried in piles of miscellaneous stuff. You will never be able to see where the homeowner is reaching or be sure there won't be a gun there. As we clear an area the piles will move and a gun that had been pointed toward the ceiling can shift and now be in a position to hurt someone.

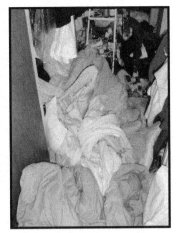

I've noticed over the years that many of my clients tend to pick a spot to "nest" in. They eat, watch TV and sleep in the same chair, spot on the couch, or pile of blankets. In this picture you can see the nest the client set up in a doorway. This means that any knives they have used to eat their dinners are often right there next to them. One day I was at a client's house and I sat down on the couch. I stood up immediately because I had sat on a steak knife which was between the couch cushions. The knife went into my butt cheek deeply enough that it still hung there when I stood up. This is why I now only sit on hard furniture in a client's home whenever possible. Had the client been angry this knife would have been in easy reach and I could have felt it in a very different way.

Hypodermic needles aren't necessarily a weapon, but they are a definite hazard to be aware of. It's possible that the homeowner is addicted to something illegal, but it's more likely that the needles are for medicinal use. Their hoard is their addiction. In a home with a normal amount of clutter these needles are usually kept near the medicine in a convenient and logical location, even if they are hidden from view. Sharps containers are usually used and are replaced regularly. In a hoarded environment those needles could be anywhere, including in the middle of that pile you need to grab hold of or lean on to keep your balance.

Pets

If you are allergic, I will assume you are medicating to handle the normal levels of pets that you are likely to find in a home since you will be going into "normal" pet containing houses all the time. If there were ever pets in a hoarded home it will not have a normal level of allergens. You can assume there will be several years' worth of pet fur and dander on the floor and in the air. Even people without allergies can find themselves reacting in this environment.

Pets are wonderful to have in a family. They are there to bring us joy, to comfort and protect us. They read our moods and respond. As an outsider, this can be a real problem for you, especially if you're the one making their person anxious and unhappy.

Imagine that you are inside a hoarded home and you are condemning it. You are explaining to the owner why he has to leave it. The homeowner is angry and upset and getting more so by the minute. All these emotions are picked up by Fluffy who only wants to defend his person and make him feel better, preferably by getting rid of the source of the negative emotions, you.

Fluffy is defending his turf and may actually be cornered with nowhere to go. He starts acting aggressively. You want to retreat but you can't move out of his way since there is only this one path in or out and you certainly don't want to turn your back on him. The homeowner usually will either not realize how upset the dog is or worse, will egg the dog on. Now you are dealing with a person you can't trust not to come at you with a weapon as well as the teeth and claws of the dog.

Cats never really care about the stuff in a home. They will wander everywhere, whether in a hoarded home or one with a usual amount of clutter, but since there is more stuff, they are likely to be at a higher vantage point than you are used to.

A cat lover who hoards things may or may not hoard pets. If there are a lot of cats in a house they are usually much more aggressive. They may have gone completely feral, in which case they will fight each other and anyone or anything that they see as invading their space.

If you know there are cats in a hoarded home you will either not see them at all or you are likely to be pounced on from a high perch. If they attack, be aware that the odds are slim their vaccinations are up to date so you are looking at some potential disease issues from scratches and bites. Even if the cat is friendly, it is now a tripping hazard since you don't have space to move around it. It is amazing how much space a stretched out cat can take up and if they are in the only walking space, it's a problem.

Cats will also mark their territories with their waste. When there are litter boxes, they are often overflowing and have an ammonia smell so strong that even the cats don't want to go near them. This level of ammonia is also dangerous to people and you may find your breathing becomes difficult and your eyes may begin to water which can lead to partially obstructed vision. The homeowners are used to this and so will not have the same reactions. This puts you at a disadvantage.

Animal hoarding was discussed in Chapters 8 and 11 but here you need to remember that the animals have usually not been socialized and so will not react well to people. As a stranger and a potential threat, the aggression toward you will be much higher. You are also likely to encounter animals who are injured or who have been killed by others due to them going feral. Most jurisdictions do not have a limit on the number of cats a person can own so you may have to get them out using the Animal Cruelty statutes in your region. If you know there is animal hoarding on a property, you may want to ensure that your local Animal Control Officer or the ASPCA is there to round up and care for the animals when you go in.

Pests

Mice and rats - Most homes have a mouse or two occasionally. They will get in when the weather turns cool, looking for a warm place to stay. The usual homeowner will get them out one way or another as soon as they know about it. In a hoarded home, the resident doesn't usually know they have a problem until there is a full infestation. They are in the walls, under the  floors, in the attic and in and amongst all the stuff. In the house pictured, the owner told me when we started that there could be a couple of mice in the house and maybe a squirrel in the attic. There were lots of mouse holes and poop all through the house. It was just under everything and he couldn't see the damage that was happening in his home. In the Clutter Hoarding Scale there is a description of the different levels but I think of it like this.... Level 1 – you may see some evidence of mice, the occasional dropping, a quick glimpse as it runs and hides. Level 3 – you hear or see them while you are in the room and they don't seem afraid. Level 5 – they are looking at you as if asking "What are you doin' in MY house?" Rats will defend their territory from all comers, including the humans who own the place. Vermin also carry fleas, mites and ticks that can carry infectious diseases to humans so even if the rat doesn't get you, his parasites can. Squirrels are just rats with bushy tails so all the same problems apply and they can be even more aggressive.

Wildlife - Raccoons and possums are really dangerous to deal with. They will defend themselves and their territory ferociously. They are prone to rabies and other diseases. If you know any of these are in a home you should call in animal control right away and stay as far away from them as possible.

Snakes - While I am not a huge fan of snakes, I would rather work in a house with snakes than with mice or rats. Yes, the snakes keep the vermin population down, but more importantly, they only attack people if they don't have a way out. As long as you stomp around and give them time to escape, you will usually not even see them. They do not carry the parasites that can harm people so at least there is one less thing to worry about.

Insects and bugs - I was contacted by a Geriatric Care Manager who told me that she had a client and when she was approaching the house for the first time the pest control guy was just leaving. He told her not to enter because the house had roaches "of biblical proportions" and it would not be safe for her to go in. He had just done a treatment and he hoped that, given the clutter providing so much food and so many hiding places, he could get them under control within 6 – 9 months, but he wasn't sure if he could. Clutter is an oasis for insects.

Most people these days are scared and creeped out by bedbugs. Don't be. Bedbugs are nocturnal so you're not likely to see them active. They nest near their food source, the homeowner, but tend to nest in corners or the underside of cushions. You're not there to clean the place up so you're not likely to be disturbing their nests. And best of all, bedbugs are not known to carry any human communicable diseases. I'm not saying to invite the little bugger home with you, but don't be afraid of being in someone else's house with them. If the homeowner appears to be itchy or has a mild skin rash, light scratches or several tiny red dots there has probably been something biting him. It's most likely fleas, but it could be lice or bedbugs. Just inspect yourself when you leave to make sure you didn't pick any up.

I'm sure you know that a termite infestation causes structural damage but unfortunately, you won't know about it until something fails. Sometimes a floor that feels spongy is a result of water damage but sometimes it is insect damage. Either way, extreme care is called for.

13 HOW TO INTERACT WITH SOMEONE WHO HOARDS

The most important thing to remember when working with someone who appears to be hoarding is that your reaction sets the tone for the entire interaction. If you go into the situation being disgusted and judgmental you will get a very negative response back and an unwillingness to cooperate with you. This will not get you the results you are looking for and will waste a lot of time and resources. If you go in with a friendly attitude you are much more likely to be successful in helping the resident as well as helping to cut down on their recidivism rate and court time. This doesn't mean you shouldn't set firm goals and timelines, it's more about keeping a professional attitude. You can be encouraging while setting limits and keeping your distance. Of course, if you don't see much improvement you may have to be more stern in your demeanor or goal setting but you will need to maintain that open line of communication to see any chance of improvement.

One thing people can find it very difficult to wrap their head around is the fact that just because a person hoards doesn't mean they are a bad person, parent, spouse or child. They are not stupid and they are not willfully causing everyone problems.

<u>What are They Thinking?</u>

People who are hoarding don't live like this because they want to. They are often embarrassed and unhappy about it. This embarrassment can lead to anger including striking out, tears, and even hopelessness. "Why should I bother?" "Just take it all, I know I don't matter", "Just kill me now and get it over with." They may not answer questions or follow your directions. This is not because they are being difficult, it's because they <u>can't</u>.

You may ask the person to stand in the doorway while you look around and when you turn around they are right behind you. It's not because they are willfully not listening, it's because their concern about what you are doing to their things pulled them to where you are.

They don't understand why they are being picked on. They will often tell me that if I go to any house on the block I will see how everyone lives like this, they are no different from their neighbors. Someone must be out to get them. They also believe that as an adult they have the right to live however they please and no one has the right to tell them how clean their house has to be. This level of defensiveness can make them seem bull-headed and can make them difficult to work with. These arguments are simply the way they are attempting to defend themselves against you, not a lack of respect.

Location, Location, Location

Just being in a cluttered environment can make anyone anxious, even when it's their stuff. It can up your anxiety and possibly make you shorter tempered than you would be normally. You should pay attention to your reactions both to the homeowner and the environment.

Now imagine how that owner might feel having you, an official, in their environment. They will most likely feel that every time you are looking at something you are judging them. Their anxiety levels will probably be high and they may not respond the way you would expect or as well as they would in a less stressful environment.

It is often best to remove yourself and the client from the cluttered environment. A local coffee shop is good but even just being out on the front porch or taking a walk can really help.

- Reduces stress levels
- Removes the person from easy reach of a weapon
- Many people talk more freely when moving. I have found that walking next to someone means that you are not eye to eye so there is less stress and the client feels less cornered. They can also talk about more emotional things without losing control if they don't feel like their every expression is being watched and evaluated. This works with spouses and children, too, when a difficult conversation is necessary.

Obviously, if you are in uniform they may not want to have you standing on their front porch or taking them for a walk. Also, if the porch is hoarded it may not be the best location as you won't get the relaxation you are looking for since you are still surrounded by all their stuff.

Time Frame

You also need to remember the time frame. The house didn't get hoarded overnight and won't be fixed overnight. This is not a short term problem. It takes time to retrain a person's habits. Expect a behavior change to take months or years.

The TV shows demonstrate what is called a "Forced Cleanout." Obviously this is effective since the home is cleared out in 2 days but the psychological damage done to the homeowner is profound. Statistically, homes that were cleaned out in this way look as bad or worse 4 months after they did the cleanout. The homeowner will do whatever it takes to re-fill the home to regain their feeling of safety and comfort. Since there was obviously not enough or you could not have taken it all away, they must need more. They will pick up items from the side of the road, make thrift store purchases, and hunt down free item listings on craigslist and similar locations. This makes refilling the house happen very quickly. The desire to reacquire is so strong that some have even been known to steal.

Recidivism rates are high – almost 100% without therapy and 70-90% with it. If in therapy, interventions tend to happen sooner with slower rates of re-hoarding. It's kind of like a roller coaster where each hill is shorter than the one before. If properly managed, backsliding will happen less drastically and less often each time, ultimately leading to a new lifestyle, one that is safe for the client and they can maintain.

The Family

The family is often on both sides of this problem. There is usually a lot of anger and frustration in the household and tempers can be short. There might be fights over lost bill payments, foreclosures, and utilities that are turned off. Someone who self soothes by shopping may make it impossible to pay the bills. This frustration is sometimes taken out on the children or elders in the home, whether they are the ones hoarding or not.

Unfortunately, not only are family members targets of this aggression, but the officials who have to deal with them often take the brunt of the anger, too. "Why are you picking on my mom?" "Who do you think you are to come into our home and tell us what to do?" Sometimes people find it easier to blame the outsider, especially if they represent the government in some way, than the family member. This applies even if they yell at the family member all the time about this stuff, everyone turns on the common enemy, you. This makes the usually dangerous Domestic Violence scenario even more dangerous.

Often there are multiple people in the home who are hoarding. Recent research shows that 80% of children raised in hoarded homes begin to hoard themselves. Some of this is the biological predisposition we talked about earlier as well as the environment they were raised in.

The "Do"s and "Don't"s of Working with the Hoarding Person

Don't

o Say "Just do it." If they could, they would have already. This is not a choice they are making, it is a problem they need help to fix.

o Nag. Calling every day to ask "Did you do anything today?" is not going to help. This is not to say that you don't have to set timelines and give them tasks to help them meet your goals but you don't have to be on them every minute. One bad example was the Code Officer who saw one of his hoarding cases in the grocery store and he stopped her to ask why she was shopping rather than cleaning up her house. She was there to buy food for her family but got so flustered she left and due to being upset she didn't have the energy to work on the house and the kids had no milk for their breakfast.

o   Talk down to the person. These are not erring children. These are grown adults who do not have the skills they need but they do have personal dignity you should respect.

o   Ridicule or criticize the person. Calling names or being harsh will only drive them to acquire and hold on to more possessions as a way to self soothe and to protect themselves from you.

o   Exaggerate the consequences. I have seen family members tell their 85 year old parent that they were going to be put in jail for the rest of their lives if they didn't get the house cleaned up in a week. Once the person learns this isn't true, they won't believe anything they are told, even when the information is correct.

o   Act shocked or as if this is insane. This is difficult to do but this is <u>normal</u> to this person. They don't know this is an extreme behavior or what your problem is. If you act like they are crazy or if you appear shocked they will shut down and won't work with you to improve. It's obvious to them that you are against them, don't understand and probably never will.

o   Ask <u>WHY</u>? This question will set you back faster than any other. I have tried to eliminate "why" from my language when working with hoarding clients. If someone asks you a why question the usual result is that defensive barriers go up and people stop listening. If I were to ask my son why he did something, his usual response would be "I dunno." This isn't very helpful for either of us. With the person who's hoarding there are other problems as well. The word "why" takes the person out of the present and takes them into the past to the time they acquired the item and reinforces the reasons why they got it in the first place. "Why" also forces them to justify having kept the item for all this time. Once justified, it is much harder to get them to let go, because it now has new meaning to them.

A better approach is to ask non-Why questions which will get you real answers and not put up the barriers. Here are a few alternatives to why that we use all the time.
*   What does keeping this do for you?
*   Does keeping that help you move forward toward your goal?
*   What benefit is there to keeping this?
*   Can we set some rules for what to keep and what to let go?

- How many is a reasonable number of those to keep?

  With shoes I start with Imelda Marcos and her shoe collection on one side and 1 pair on the other extreme to establish that there is a range. Then I work with them to narrow down the range.
- What purpose does this serve for you?

<u>Do</u>

o Even though it can be tough, find something to compliment them on during every visit. It can be a painting they uncovered while decluttering, the fact that you can see improvement in this area and it's looking better, etc. You need to provide the carrot as well as the stick for best improvement.

o Recognize that they are embarrassed and would really prefer you were not seeing their situation. They are afraid they are in legal trouble and could be going to jail just by letting you come in the front door. You are a danger to them. They have heard horror stories much of their lives about how someone got thrown in jail for not cleaning up. What they <u>didn't</u> hear was how many years it took to get to that point, how many extensions the person got, and how much help there were offered or received. They only heard the bad final result.

o The code infractions that are being enforced are usually listed on the citation but these are often not in language the citizenry understands. While the Federal Government has regulations for plain language for the IRS and Insurance companies, those rules have not been adopted for most local Property Maintenance Codes. Most homeowners will need to get an explanation of what your expectations are before you consider them to be compliant. It would be a good idea to create a punch list for them of everything they need to do. Many Inspectors give a very short list and then add on the next step. To the homeowner it feels like things are being added on for no reason, they don't understand the short list was to help keep them from being overwhelmed. If the list is complete, then they can see what they have accomplished and what is left to do.

o Act as if their situation is normal, since it is to them. Be matter of fact – say you have seen worse, even if you never have. You can use the TV shows about hoarding and animal hoarding as mental images if it helps. In my case, even if I have never seen so much clutter, at least it's not as bad in terms of squalor so I have seen worse. If there is a lot of waste, at least there isn't a dead body here. You get the idea – there is always something worse in some way or another. In your lines of work it should be fairly easy to find something that was nastier in some way than what you are looking at.

o Realize that their emotions are represented by their "stuff". Each pile is a pile of anger, sadness, hopelessness, or fear. It's never really about the stuff, it about what the stuff represents.

o Keep in mind your own safety, but give them your full attention when they are speaking so they feel as though you are not criticizing their environment. They will notice if you are looking around and they will assume you are not listening to them and you are judging them. This will cause them to shut down which means they won't listen to you and won't work on the home.

o Listen without judgment and with an open mind. This does not mean you have to let them do what they want. If you keep an open mind you are likely to hear the things that will trigger them and you can use those triggers to help them improve. For example, if Bob is talking about how much he loves spending time with the grandkids, you can use them to motivate him to clean up the living room so the kids can come over. If you go in closed off you will miss all those clues and it will make your job much more difficult and the interaction rougher than it has to be.

o Remember, sometimes you are "The Heavy" an organizer or therapist will need to use to get the client moving. I will usually say to the client at the beginning of the process that I understand their goal is to get you off their back. Later on as they are showing progress we can take a friendlier attitude but sometimes the only way to get help in there is to be "Us versus Them." Work with the therapist and organizer to know when you can be encouraging and when you have to be the heavy. If there is no outside assistance you will need to keep a firm line but make sure you notice whatever improvement there is and encourage more of it.

o Understand that the hoarding person is often alone. Friends and family have abandoned them, usually with a lot of name calling, shaming and sometimes violence. Hoarding is how they protect themselves and stay safe so you are ordering them to break down their safety walls with no net under them. This is incredibly difficult.

o Realize that you can be dealing with true Hoarding Disorder or Chronic Disorganization. These two groups can react very differently to the same words/attitudes. Pay close attention.

o Be aware of the comorbid disorders we explored in Chapter 10. These will have a PROFOUND effect on the citizen's ability to organize, make decisions on what to keep, what to donate and where to donate them. Things will take much longer but once new behaviors and skills are learned there can be good progress.

What Can the Type of Clutter Tell You About How to Work with the Citizen?

Back in Chapter 2 we talked about several types of clutter. Understanding these types can help you to understand the person who's hoarding and how to motivate them.

- ## Paper and Information Hoarding

  People with a lot of paper, magazines, books, etc. often see themselves as intellectuals and smarter than the average person. Even if their beliefs are out of the norm (conspiracy theorists, etc) they believe that they are part of the elite. They are willing to prove this to you at every opportunity, so unless your desire is to spend the entire day with them getting nowhere, don't engage in the discussion in the first place.

  You can try the logical approach with them.

  > "Do you realize the damage that this is causing to the house from its weight and how much it will cost to repair?"

  > "If you went digital you could have all this info at your fingertips no matter where you are in the world."

- ## Clothing and Sentimental

  People with a lot of clothing or sentimental items are living in the past. While some people will keep a set of "Fat clothes" most people keep clothes one, two or more sizes too small. This attachment to clothing that don't fit or is out of date, like the sentimental collector, hearken back to a past life. Nothing in the past looks as bad now as it did then.

  You can try the current life approach with them as well as a greater good angle with them.

  > "I know you are hoping to lose the weight but if these clothes don't fit you, why don't you donate them to people who need them now? Once you lose the weight you can get new things that will fit you then."

  > "Are there one or two items which are the most important and can represent the whole collection? You could put those in a shadow box and they wouldn't take up any floor space. You could put a swatch of your mom's wedding dress and one of your dad's suit in a frame with their wedding picture. That way, you will always have a remembrance of them

and maybe you can let go of the rest of the stuff that's just taking up space."

- **Crafts and Home Improvement**

These people are looking toward a perfect future. They chase the ideal and will be distracted by the new great idea they just had. They will be disjointed and will tell you about how useful the item is or all the cool stuff they can do with this one, no matter that it has been sitting there waiting to be used for the last 15 years.

Try a reality check with them.

> "Let's look at the last 3 projects you told me about. How many hours will each one take to complete if you started right now? How many hours a day do you have to work on them? If each one will take 40 hours to complete and you only have 1 hour a day to spend, you will take 4 months to complete these three jobs. Do you think you might like to take off a night here and there? Could you possibly get sick? Could the kids be sick and keep you from working? If so, let's add another month. Now we're at 5 months for these 3 projects and you told me you have over 100 projects. Are there any projects you could let go of because they don't hold your interest any more? Can you limit yourself to X number of projects and let the less important ones go?"

- **Collections**

To some extent, the type of collection makes the difference. If they collect dolls, they want to make connections with people and things. If they collect coins, it's more like the future worth collector. Look carefully at the collection and try to see what the root emotional need it is representing and respond accordingly.

If it is a goal to connect with people and things, suggest an alternative solution.

> "Have you considered reading to children/elders/the blind to give you more time interacting with others?"

> "You say that you miss your children, have
> you considered volunteering at an elementary school as a room mom?"

- **Animals**

These folks can be attached to a pet which is now deceased and may be holding on to the paraphernalia because of that attachment, or they may have just not thought to get rid of the items.

The "reasonable number" argument can work here.

> "What do you think is a reasonable number of leashes (bowls, toys, etc) to have for one dog?"

> "If you now only have small dogs, do you still need to have the large crate and food bowls? "

- **Accidental Collections**

These people don't even know why they have these things so are often baffled as to what they should do with them.

Try the donation route

> "Since you don't know what you are going to do with all those stress balls, how about you donate them to the local family shelter, or the Boy's Club. The kids will love throwing them at each other."

- **Bargains, Future Worth**

These are the future millionaires in the group. They have been saving metal, coins, whatever so that when they retire they can do so in STYLE!!

Try the reality check here

> "OK, you are keeping this metal to pay for your retirement. Let's see how much you have here. Let's estimate the weight, the amount you get per pound and the cost of hauling to the recycling center." If they say they will use their own truck, figure out the gas and wear and tear (use IRS amount so it doesn't seem like you are making up the numbers). Do the subtraction and see what is left. Then subtract the repairs to the back yard. "Is it worth it? How much are you losing to rust? "

> "You bought these commemorative plates as an investment. What are they worth on ebay right now?" Make sure you check what they actually sold for, not what people are asking. The later will give you a highly inflated price

- ### Trash, Recycling, Boxes

  This is a very hard group to work with because you can usually start people in the right direction by having them get rid of trash. If they are hoarding trash you don't have as good of a starting point. If the issue is recycling, suggest that they take a tour of the local recycling plant. This may make them feel better about what can be recycled and how it's done. If they won't go, you will have to set VERY clear guidelines and expect a lot of push-back.

  Try the education track by having them take the tour or read the local center's literature

- ### Invisible

  Since they literally don't see the problem, it can be difficult to get them to work on it. You may have to jar them out of their reality by showing them what's there in an unusual way.

  Try taking photos and showing them the pictures when not in the space. Also try draping. With draping you take a white sheet and block off around a pile. It makes the pile independent of the rest of the visual clutter and they will be more likely to "see" it. This technique also helps clear the space since you aren't as distracted by the other things in the vicinity.

Stages of Dealing with Someone that Hoards

I was reading one of the fact sheets by ICD (FS007) and they listed 4 stages for communicating with Chronically Disorganized people. This resonated with me because I had noticed that sometimes I felt these things so I have expanded on it here.

Often you will deal with the same person several times. This can be over several years or several rounds of citation and cleanup. If so, you will probably go through these stages – possibly more than once. These also don't happen in any particular order, you can jump from one to the other like a ping-pong ball. I'll give an example of each in order but you can vacillate between several stages in a single appointment.

To explain the stages we will look at Margaret and her daughter Peg. Margaret's kitchen is really cluttered and Peg has come over to help.

- • **Stage 1** – offering encouragement

  This is the "Cheerleader" phase. Peg's reaction is "OK Mom, let's tackle this kitchen and together we'll have it sparkling and clean in no time!" No, I am not the gung-ho, bouncy type but I keep a "We can do this together" attitude that accomplishes the same thing

Now Peg goes back to Margaret's house and the kitchen is messy again.

- **<u>Stage 2</u>** – Being disappointed with failures and backsliding

    This is the "I love you but don't like what you have done" phase. "Mom, you told me when I helped you clean this up last time that you would keep it clean. I'll help you again but please just keep it clean this time." If you picture this with a long-suffering sigh and a little pleading in the voice you can see how this would go.

Again the kitchen gets messy

- **<u>Stage 3</u>** - Irritation with the rate of progress

    This is the "angry parent" phase. "Mom! The last time I was over here and helped you, you said that you would keep it clean! I don't have time to waste over here all the time picking up after you! I have a husband and kids and while I will help you ONE MORE TIME, you had better not let it get messy again!!!"

And finally,

- **<u>Stage 4</u>** – Withdrawing to avoid expressing anger

    This is the "I'm DONE" phase. Most of our hoarding clients have children that do not talk to them, never visit and who won't allow any contact with the grandchildren.

Margaret isn't a bad person. She has a problem, but she is a kind and loving lady who has now been abandoned. The better response for Peg would be to see her mom outside of the home and to try to keep a relationship with her. She doesn't need to condone the behavior but if she can stay involved with her mom there is a greater likelihood of success in therapy and in making the necessary changes.

It is very difficult to stay in Stage 1. When I find myself sliding into the later stages I talk to someone else who will understand and support me – my husband, another organizer or a "Paid Friend" aka a therapist. This lets me re-center so I go back into that situation in a positive mindset.

14 RESOURCES FOR THE PERSON WHO HOARDS

The more resources you can offer the citizen the better. Not everything works for everyone but having a few of these in your back pocket will make your job a lot easier. Don't get locked into what the County you work in can provide, see what's out there in the private sector. If your county has a Hoarding Task Force, invite the appropriate businesses in to help. You can also create a resource list to share among all the affected departments with providers that have been helpful in the past.

SUPPORT SYSTEMS

- Friends and Family – can be a tremendous resource for support but they MUST be coached on what to do and say as well as what NOT to do or say. This coaching is best done by an organizer or therapist who specializes in hoarding.

- Therapist – Make sure to find one with a sincere interest in the disorder. A bad therapist is worse than none sometimes. Do not assume that they will understand the complexities of the situation if this isn't something that really speaks to them. Remember CBT has been the most effective methodology so far.

- Charities – good source for volunteers. This is particularly useful if there is a very short deadline and a forced cleanout is needed. This can be done with less damage to the homeowner when properly managed but it is still a last resort.

- Religious organizations – support for the homeowner both with the clean out and with the emotional support. Often church members will offer to run trash to the dump or take donations to charity as a way to save the homeowners money. They will need proper training if they will be entering the home and touching items. In many places confirmation classes have a service requirement and this could be a good way to use them.

- Professional Organizers – There are several specialties for organizers (see Appendix 4) The one group that is really needed but may be the most difficult for a client to hire is the hoarding specialist. In order to look for a hoarding specialist the person has to admit a need for one and this is an extremely difficult thing to do. This specialist should be able to clearly explain how they work, what experience they have, and what continuing training they are getting. The field has changed so much in the last 10 years, if the organizer isn't staying up to date they may be using techniques which are less effective and may be harmful.

SELF DIAGNOSTIC QUIZZES

- Many fact sheets are available on the ICD site under the publications tab: http://www.challengingdisorganization.org/node/112

- Current and Past ICD Research Projects – ICD sponsors and collaborates in on-going research. If you are interested in past studies or participating in one, visit: http://www.challengingdisorganization.org/content/icd-research

SUPPORT GROUPS AND 12 STEP PROGRAMS

- Local Workshops - ie. Buried in Treasures

- ACOH buddies (Adult Children of Hoarders) – www.childrenofhoarders.com

- Overcoming Hoarding Together – http://health.groups.yahoo.com/group/O-H-T/

- Compulsive Hoarding Community – https://groups.yahoo.com/neo/groups/H-C/info

The following are less hoarding specific but still an option

- Clutterers Anonymous http://clutterersanonymous.org/

- Clutterless Recovery Groups http://clutterless.org/

- Clutter Buddies http://clutterbuddies.org

- MESSIES Anonymous www.messies.com

THERAPY

- County Mental Health Services – if they can't help they may know of other organizations that can assist low income residents.

- Local Therapists – some have a sliding scale and due to the changes to the new DSM – 5 these services may be covered by insurance.

- Harm Reduction International website - www.ihra.net

PROFESSIONAL ORGANIZERS

- Institute for Challenging Disorganization - www.challengingdisorganization.org

- National Association of Professional Organizers www.napo.net

BOOKS

Ghosty Men: The strange but true story of the Collyer brothers and my Uncle Arthur, New York's Greatest Hoarders (Lidz)

The Hoarding Handbook: A guide for Human Service Professionals (Bratiotis, Schmalisch and Steketee)

What Every Professional Organizer* Needs to Know About Hoarding (Kolberg)

What Every Professional Organizer* Needs to Know About Chronic Disorganization (Kolberg)

Stuff: Compulsive Hoarding and the Meaning of Things (Steketee and Frost)

Buried in Treasures: Help for Compulsive Acquiring, Saving, and Hoarding (Tolin, Frost, Steketee)

Digging Out: Helping Your Loved One Manage Clutter, Hoarding and Compulsive Acquiring (Tompkins, Hartl)

Overcoming Compulsive Hoarding: Why You Save and How You Can Stop (Neziroglu, Bubrick, Yaryura-Tobias)

Compulsive Hoarding and Acquiring: Therapist Manual (Steketee, Frost)

Compulsive Hoarding and Acquiring: Workbook (Steketee, Frost)

Manage Clutter, Hoarding and Compulsive Acquiring (Tompkins, Hartl)

The Hoarder in You: How to live a happier, healthier, uncluttered life (Zasio)

The Secret Lives of Hoarders (Paxton)

ICD Guide to Challenging Disorganization: For Professional Organizers (ICD)

ICD Guide to Collaborating with Professional Organizers: For Related Professionals (ICD)

Life at Home in the Twenty-first Century: 32 Families Open Their Doors (Jeanne)

Cognitive Approaches to Obsessions and Compulsions: Theory, Assessment, and Treatment (Frost and Steketee)

Overcoming Compulsive Hoarding: Why you save & How you can stop (Neziroglu)

Don't Toss my Memories in the Trash (Dellaquila)

ANIMAL HOARDING

- Tufts University Hoarding of Animals Research Consortium
  http://vet.tufts.edu/hoarding/

- Humane Society of the United States
  http://www.humanesociety.org/animals/pets/

- American Vetrerinary Medical Foundation
  www.avma.org

ONLINE MENTAL HEALTH ARTICLES REFERENCED

- International Code Council - www.**icc**safe.org
- http://www.compulsive-hoarding.org/About.html
- http://psychiatry.ucsd.edu/OCD_hoarding.html
- http://www.nhs.uk/Conditions/hoarding/Pages/Introduction.aspx
- www.nhs.uk/Conditions/Obsessive-compulsive-disorder/Pages/Causes.aspx
- http://ajp.psychiatryonline.org/article.aspx?articleid=98001

- http://www.socialworkblog.org/practice-and-professional-development/2008/07/is-hoarding-a-big-deal/ *(There is another article inside this one on getting an Ex back)*
- http://www.anxietyandstress.com/#!hoarding/c1vny

APPENDIX 1 DSM-5 ALTERATIONS FOR THE INCLUSION OF HOARDING DISORDER AS A SEPARATE DIAGNOSIS

- Hoarding disorder graduates from being listed as just one symptom of obsessive-compulsive personality disorder in the DSM-IV, to a full-blown diagnostic category in the DSM-5. After the DSM-5 OCD working group examined the research literature on hoarding, they found little support to suggest this was simply a variant of a personality disorder, or a component of another mental disorder.

- **Hoarding disorder is characterized by the persistent difficulty discarding or parting with possessions, regardless of the value others may attribute to these possessions, according to the APA's new criteria:**

- The behavior **usually has harmful effects** — emotional, physical, social, financial, and even legal — for the person suffering from the disorder and family members. For individuals who hoard, the quantity of their collected items sets them apart from people with normal collecting behaviors. They accumulate a large number of possessions that often fill up or clutter active living areas of the home or workplace to the extent that their intended use is no longer possible.

- Symptoms of the disorder cause **clinically significant distress or impairment** in social, occupational or other important areas of functioning including maintaining an environment for self and/or others. While some people who hoard may not be particularly distressed by their behavior, their behavior can be distressing to other people, such as family members or landlords.

- Hoarding disorder is included in DSM-5 because research shows that it is a distinct disorder with distinct treatments. Using DSM-IV, individuals with pathological hoarding behaviors could receive a diagnosis of obsessive-compulsive disorder (OCD), obsessive-compulsive personality disorder, anxiety disorder not otherwise specified or no diagnosis at all, since many severe cases of hoarding are not accompanied by obsessive or compulsive behavior. Creating a unique diagnosis in DSM-5 will increase public awareness, improve identification of cases, and stimulate both research and the development of specific treatments for hoarding disorder.

- This is particularly important as studies show that the prevalence of hoarding disorder is estimated at approximately two to five percent of the population. These behaviors can often be quite severe and even threatening. Beyond the mental impact of the disorder, the accumulation of clutter can create a public health issue by completely filling people's homes and creating fall and fire hazards.

Found at: http://pro.psychcentral.com/2013/dsm-5-changes-obsessive-compulsive-and-related-disorders/004404.html

APPENDIX 2 DEFINITIONS OF AGENCIES AND TERMS

Animal = Animal Control. Their job is to ensure animals are not being abused or neglected. They often run a local animal shelter for strays where people can adopt animals. Some areas rely on non-governmental agencies such as the ASPCA.

ADD/ADHD = As defined by the Mayo Clinic: Attention-deficit/hyperactivity disorder (ADHD) is a chronic condition that affects millions of children and often continues into adulthood. ADHD includes a combination of persistent problems, such as difficulty sustaining attention, hyperactivity and impulsive behavior.Children with ADHD also may struggle with low self-esteem, troubled relationships and poor performance in school. Symptoms sometimes lessen with age. However, some people never completely outgrow their ADHD symptoms. But they can learn strategies to be successful.

ADL = Activities of Daily Living. These are mostly the concern of APS. This is the list of extremely basic activities a person needs to be able to accomplish on their own to be considered able to live unassisted. These include Bathing, Dressing, Feeding themselves, Transferring from one seat to another and Toileting. More advanced things like handling money are IADL's and are not discussed here.

APS = Adult Protective Services. Their job is to assist those over the age of 60, or over 18 if disabled, by protecting them from abuse or neglect. Unlike CPS, they do not have the ability to forcibly remove an adult from their situation. People assume they have the same powers which can sometimes lead to more compliance than the citizen would give if they knew the truth. They are also often mandated reporters and so will call in the police, Social Services or CMT.

Churning = The mixing of the important with the unimportant. This is usually a result of trying to keep the most important things on the top of the pile to make remembering them easier. Since there are more important things than there is space, piles keep being shifted and items are lost. This leads to even more frantic searches and pile shifting while looking.

CPS = Child Protective Services. Their task is to protect children from abusive or neglectful situations. They have the independent authority to remove children from the home and can prevent the parents or others from access to the children.

CMT = Crisis Management Team. Their job is to respond to immediate requests to determine if a citizen can care for themselves or if they are a danger to themselves or others. They are often part of another group such as the Police Department or Mental Health Services instead of being independent.

Code = Code Compliance. Their job is to ensure the buildings we citizens enter: residential, commercial, and industrial, are safe. They do things like conducting plumbing and electrical inspections during construction, as well as inspecting afterward to ensure compliance with the Property Maintenance Codes. The latter includes things like clear egress, fire hazards, and structural damage.

EMT = Emergency Medical Technician. Their job is to render emergency medical aide, often including transportation of the victim to the hospital. They carry approx 80 lbs of equipment into the average job, not including transportation devices like a gurney.

Fire = Fire Marshalls. Their job is to make sure that the fire safety codes are enforced to allow citizens as well as fire fighters and EMT's able to fight fires and help in medical situations safely while carrying all their necessary equipment.

HOA = Home Owners Association. This is a private group whose goal is to ensure certain minimum standards are maintained in a community. This can include maintenance, paint colors, landscaping, etc. The reason for this oversight is to ensure that one person's home appearance cannot bring down the property values for his neighbors.

Housing = Housing and Community Development. In some communities this department does much of the code compliance work that does NOT include interior wall inspections. They look at things like exterior clutter issues and structural integrity. They are often used to assess Section 8 housing for compliance.

OCD = As defined by Psychology Today: Obsessive-compulsive disorder (OCD) is an anxiety disorder in which people have unwanted and repeated thoughts, feelings, ideas, sensations (obsessions), or behaviors that make them feel driven to do something (compulsions).Often the person carries out the behaviors to get rid of the obsessive thoughts, but this only provides temporary relief. Not performing the obsessive rituals can cause great anxiety. A person's level of OCD can be anywhere from mild to severe, but if severe and left untreated, it can destroy a person's capacity to function at work, at school or even to lead a comfortable existence in the home.

Property Maintenance Codes = There is an International set of codes for interior and exterior maintenance. (International Code Council) Each Country gets to decide which they will enforce. Then each state decides, then each county and then each city. This leads to some cities enforcing most or all and some not enforcing any.

APPENDIX 3 CLUTTER HOARDING SCALE

The scale comes in both a full-size, multipage booklet and a handy trifold. This is a free download from the Institute for Challenging Disorganization (ICD) although a donation for further research would be appreciated.

www.challengingdisorganization.org

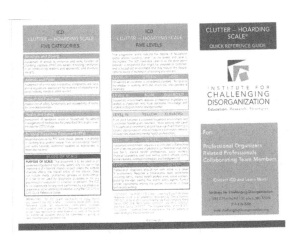

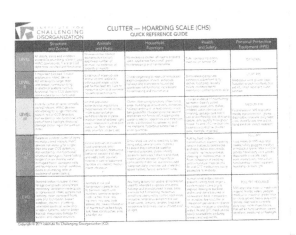

APPENDIX 4 WHAT IS A PROFESSIONAL ORGANIZER

It depends on who you ask. There is a large range of services that an organizer may offer.

A Concierge organizer is a person who will run errands like picking up dry cleaning, or putting away groceries.

Some organizers specialize in technology and they can make every gadget you've ever heard of interact with each other. It's almost like they think something and it magically happens.

Student organizers work with students of all ages to help them get and stay organized so they get the best possible results in school.

Elder specialists understand the needs of the aging population and work with their clients to make the homes safer for aging in place, help them downsize to another location, and can help them get their affairs in order for their eventual passing. This would include tasks like making sure all the legal paperwork is easy for their family to find and take over, create secure password files for online bill paying, create letters to include with legal paperwork that direct who will receive what tangible personal property and much more.

Some work with moms and their children to teach the children how to be more organized.

Hoarding specialists are usually the most difficult to hire since the client needs to admit they have a problem before they hire one. The most effective method for working with hoarding is to go slowly and to learn how to make the decisions that are best for that person. Quick clean-outs are not necessarily the best, even if they are cheaper, if they cause damage and make it more likely to re-hoard. Slow and steady is best.

When hiring a Professional Organizer, the client should make sure they are very comfortable with the person. They will be spending a lot of time with them. Look for an Organizer with a large pool of referral sources. They should be able to connect the client with reputable people to buy their items, haul their trash, and get the pests evicted. If they refer a lot of work, the companies they refer will want to keep them happy, as they are worth several clients to the service provider. This provides the client with extra clout if there is a problem.

APPENDIX 5 COST OF REMEDIATION SCENARIOS

Keep in mind that remediation is not included in this and will have a significant impact on the final costs. It also doesn't include the reduction in property values for the surrounding homes. We have simplified the scenarios here with the permission of the Mental Health Association of San Francisco.

* Text in ALL CAPS indicates new services/coordination/opportunities recommended

SCENARIO 1

Stuff piles up for "Chris." The fire exit is blocked and items are piled on the stovetop, causing a fire hazard. Chris becomes isolated. He feels panic, shame, and denial about his situation and doesn't know what to do.

Chris sees the public education and outreach on compulsive hoarding.

Chris contacts the ASSESSMENT TEAM for services.

The ASSESSMENT TEAM responds and connects Chris with SUPPORT and TREATMENT GROUP services.

After joining a SUPPORT GROUP, Chris slows his rate of acquiring and manages to clear a path to the emergency exit.

Chris joins a TREATMENT GROUP and eventually clears the top of his heater and stovetop.

Chris continues to make progress, and feels less panic, shame, and denial. He is able to stay in his housing, becomes less isolated, and starts to feel better about himself and life.

COST TOTAL SCENARIO 1 - $2,607 for one year of services.

SCENARIO 2

Stuff piles up for "Chris." The fire exit is blocked and items are piled on the stovetop, causing a fire hazard. Chris becomes isolated. He feels panic, shame, and denial about his situation and doesn't know what to do. The apartment heater stops working due to heavy boxes stacked on it. To get it fixed, Chris calls the building manager. Before the manager comes, Chris cleans, but not enough to hide the clutter. The building manager enters and repairs the heater, but recognizes that there's a larger problem with fire and safety hazards and is concerned about pest infestations.

The building manager reenters the unit to deal with the pest infestation.

The manager knows about compulsive hoarding and contacts the ASSESS-MENT TEAM. She gets advice on service options available.

The manager doesn't know what to do about the fire hazard.

SEE **SCENARIO 4**

The manager is able to give Chris CLEAR WRITTEN STANDARDS about how to come into compliance and encourages him to call the ASSESSMENT TEAM.

Chris Contacts the ASSES-SEMENT TEAM for services.

Chris is stressed and afraid, and refuses help.

The ASSESSMENT TEAM responds and connects Chris with SUPPORT, TREATMENT GROUP and cleaning services.

The landlord launches eviction proceedings.

After joining a SUPPORT GROUP, Chris slows his rate of acquiring and

SEE *SCENARIO 3* OR **SCENARIO 4** FOR COST AND STEPS

manages to clear a path   OF EVICTION
to the emergency exit.   PROCEEDINGS.

Chris joins a TREATMENT GROUP and eventually clears the top of his heater and stovetop.

Chris continues to make progress, and feels less panic, shame, and denial. He is able to stay in his housing, becomes less isolated, and starts to feel better about himself and life.

COST TOTAL SCENARIO 2 - $4,316 for one year of services. ($484 to landlord, $3,832 to social services)

SCENARIO 3

Stuff piles up for "Chris." The fire exit is blocked and items are piled on the stovetop, causing a fire hazard. Chris becomes isolated. He feels panic, shame, and denial about his situation and doesn't know what to do. The apartment heater stops working due to heavy boxes stacked on it. To get it fixed, Chris calls the building manager. Before the manager comes, Chris cleans, but not enough to hide the clutter. The building manager enters and repairs the heater, but recognizes that there's a larger problem with fire and safety hazards and is concerned about pest infestations.

The building manager reenters the unit to deal with the pest infestation.

The manager knows about compulsive hoarding and contacts the ASSESSMENT TEAM. She gets advice on service options available.

The manager is able to give Chris CLEAR WRITTEN STANDARDS about how to come into compliance and encourages him to call the ASSESSMENT TEAM.

Chris is stressed and afraid, and refuses help.

The Landlord launches eviction proceedings. (Pick up here from SCENARIO 2)

Social Services contact Chris and attempt to intervene. Chris receives legal assistance to secure reasonable accommodation.

Chris accepts some heavy cleaning over protest. He stays in his housing but is still at high risk to repeat the process

The stress has impacted Chris's health and he is now more afraid and isolated.

The landlord pays for pest control.

COST TOTAL SCENARIO 3 - $5,662 per occurrence ($1,484 to landlord, $4,178 to social services), high risk of repeat occurrence.

SCENARIO 4

Stuff piles up for "Chris." The fire exit is blocked and items are piled on the stovetop, causing a fire hazard. Chris becomes isolated. He feels panic, shame, and denial about his situation and doesn't know what to do. The apartment heater stops working due to heavy boxes stacked on it. To get it fixed, Chris calls the building manager. Before the manager comes, Chris cleans, but not enough to hide the clutter. The building manager enters and repairs the heater, but recognizes that there's a larger problem with fire and safety hazards and is concerned about pest infestations.

The building manager attempts to reenter the unit to deal with the pest infestation, but Chris panics and denies entry to her.

The pest situation worsens, and the fire hazard continues.

The manager doesn't know what to do about the fire hazard. (Pick up here from SCENARIO 2)

The landlord launches eviction proceedings.

Social Services contact Chris and attempt to intervene. Chris receives legal assistance to secure reasonable accommodation.

Chris doesn't clean or accept help and eviction results. He must now relocate.

The stress has impacted Chris's health and he is now more afraid and isolated.

The landlord pays for pest control.

COST TOTAL SCENARIO 4 - $36,880 per occurance ($26,480 to landlord, $10,400 to social services), high risk of repeat occurrence.

Examples of Financial and Social Costs of
Hoarding and Cluttering**

Comparison of each SCENARIO:

SCENARIO 1 – COST $2,607 for one year of services.
"Chris" is able to maintain his home, and receives the necessary services to improve his life and well being.

SCENARIO 2 – COST $4,316 for one year of services. The cost is increased due to lack of knowledge and awareness, the house falls into further disrepair and costs for services thereby increase.

SCENARIO 3 – COST $5,662 PER OCCURRENCE. This is not a yearly cost, this is each time the house falls below regulated standards. Again, lack of knowledge and awareness of compulsive hoarding drastically increase cost. There is no long-term benefit and REOCCURRENCE RISK IS HIGH. As no treatment has been received to resolve the cause.

SCENARIO 4 – COST $36,880 PER OCCURRENCE. Leaving "Chris" without housing, no assistance to understand compulsive hoarding and no long term benefit. The cost of eviction is devastating financially and "Chris" is left isolated, and emotionally vulnerable. REOCCURANCE RISK IS HIGH. As no treatment has been received to resolve the cause.

** This example does not include animal hoarding, which requires assistance from additional agencies, such as Animal Care and Control.

ABOUT THE AUTHOR

Maria was born and raised in NY, but is currently living in VA (because it's warmer) with her husband and their son. Maria is a collector of education, starting with a triple major in college from the business and economics department and continuing with several certifications. She receives between 60 and 80 credits per year and is greedy for more. When she's not learning, she's teaching and has been speaking on a variety of subjects nationwide for the last five and a half years.

Maria is a Volunteer In Police Service. As a VIPS she drives a canteen truck for DWI checkpoints and other events such as search and rescue and barricade events. She role plays with the Criminal Justice Academy for the cadets as well as tactical training for current Officers. As an Organizer Maria works with Code Compliance and Fire Marshals to assist citizens who are hoarding get up to code and pass inspection. She recently taught an ICD teleclass for other Professional Organizers on how to interact with Government Agencies. Over the years she has taught about Hoarding Disorder at the CJA as well as at the FBI in Quantico.

CPSIA information can be obtained
at www.ICGtesting.com
Printed in the USA
FSOW04n0645120916
24887FS